THE CONTEMPORARY Singing Actor

REVISED WOMEN'S EDITION
Volume 1

Compiled by Richard Walters

ISBN 978-0-634-04766-4

7777 W. Bluemound Rd. P.O. Box 13819 Milwaukee, WI 53213

Visit Hal Leonard Online at
www.halleonard.com

Contents by Song

Contents by Show

AROUND THE WORLD
from *Grey Gardens*

Music by SCOTT FRANKEL
Lyrics by MICHAEL KORIE

moth-er's way of re - mind-ing me if you live off moth - er, you
can't be free. So I think that moth - er is ver - y mean. And this
cresc.
Ped.
lat - est thing with this wash ma-chine? The one
Jer - ry brought. Don't be too sur-prised if the guy moves in, and I'm
mf agitato

pul-ver-ized 'cuz I'm damned if I'm gon-na waste my time wash-ing
cresc.
rall.
clothes in that god - damned ma - chine!!!!
colla voce
rall.
ff
12
Tempo di Music Box
"A-round the world" is what I call my wall of spe - cial
mp
things. "A-round the world" with rose bou - quets I dried and tied on
warmly

strings. A sil - ver mask from a mas - quer - ade a - round and 'round I
cresc.
twirled... You tack them up so you can twirl a - round the world...
dim.
Furioso
f con pedale
It's my moth - er's house and my
dim.
mp

moth-er's friends, and with Jer - ry com-ing, it nev-er ends. It's the
same old sto-ry as George Gould Strong, not in twen-ty years_ did we
get a-long! Though I do feel bad for the way he died in a
two - bit flea-bag, a su-i-cide, it was moth - er's mon-ey, the

Bou - vi - ers', and if moth - er spends it in
cresc.
5
6
Ped.
cra - zy ways, no one else took care of her,
9
mf agitato
3
on - ly me! She was tak - en care of, not "sex - ual - ly!" And if
you in - fer they were us - ing her, I will
sub. mp
cresc.

Tempo di Music Box
shove you right un-der the god-damned bed!!!!
"A-round the
Ped.
Ped.
Ped.
world" with stones and shells. The nic-est one I lost. "A-round the
mp dolce
world" with-out a boat on just a quote from Frost: "Two roads di-
warmly
verged_ in a yel-low wood." A love-ly cros - sing, all... A-round the

rall.
world, the world a - round the at - tic wall... "A-round the
cresc.
rall.
a tempo
world" there is - n't room for ev - 'ry spe - cial thing. "A-round the
f warmly
a tempo
world" you choose a few that make the mu - sic sing. A sil - ver
mp dolce
cresc.
mask from a mas-quer-ade, a-round and 'round I twirled... You tack them
mf
cresc.

rall.
up so when you go, the world will be the one you know... A
dim.
rall.
Freely
bird-cage I plan to hang... I'll get to that some-day... A bird-cage for a bird who flew a-
mp
colla voce
Poco più mosso e agitato
way... A-round the world.
14
rinforzando
p
rall.
sub. p

AS IF WE NEVER SAID GOODBYE

from *Sunset Boulevard*

Music by ANDREW LLOYD WEBBER
Lyrics by DON BLACK and CHRISTOPHER HAMPTON,
with contributions by Amy Powers

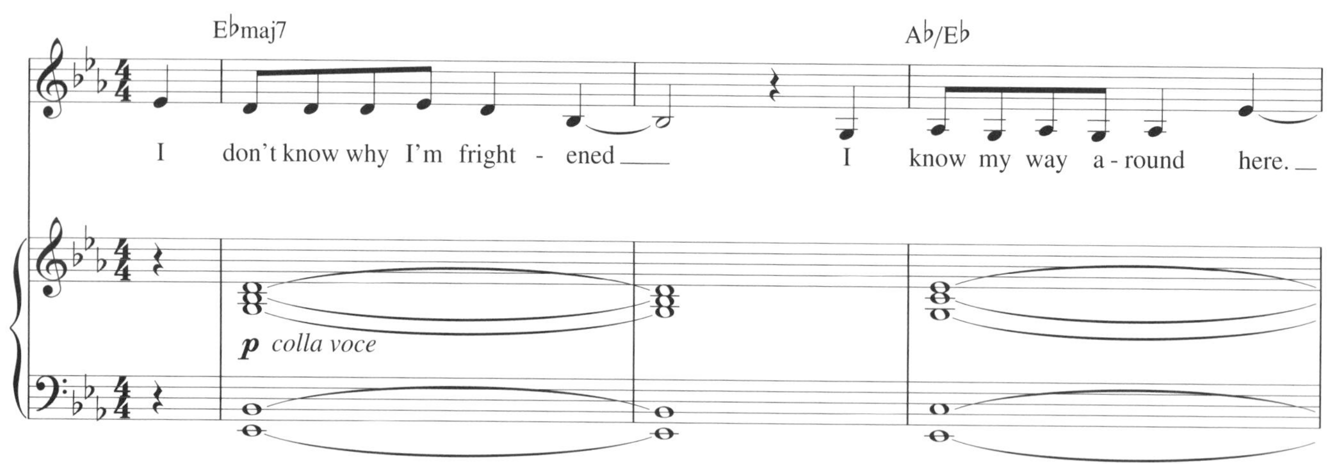

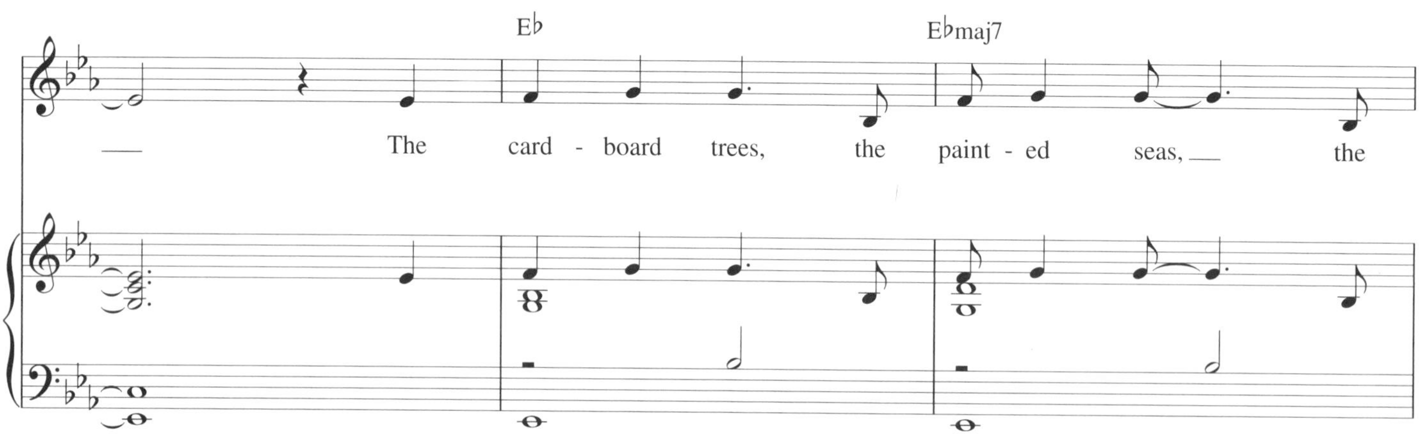

Fm7
but I'm not in an - y hur - ry, and I
D♭ A♭/C B♭7 E♭maj7
need a mo - ment. The whis - pered con - ver - sa - tions
Fm/E♭
in o - ver - crowd - ed hall - ways, the
E♭ E♭maj7 D♭maj7
at - mos - phere as thrill - ing here as al - ways.

A♭/C
Feel the ear - ly morn - ing mad - ness, feel the
Fm7
mag - ic in the mak - ing.
E♭maj7/B♭
Why, ev - 'ry - thing's as if we
A♭/B♭
nev - er said good - bye.
E♭
I've
mf
E♭maj7
spent so man - y morn - ings,
Fm/E♭
just try - ing to re - sist you.

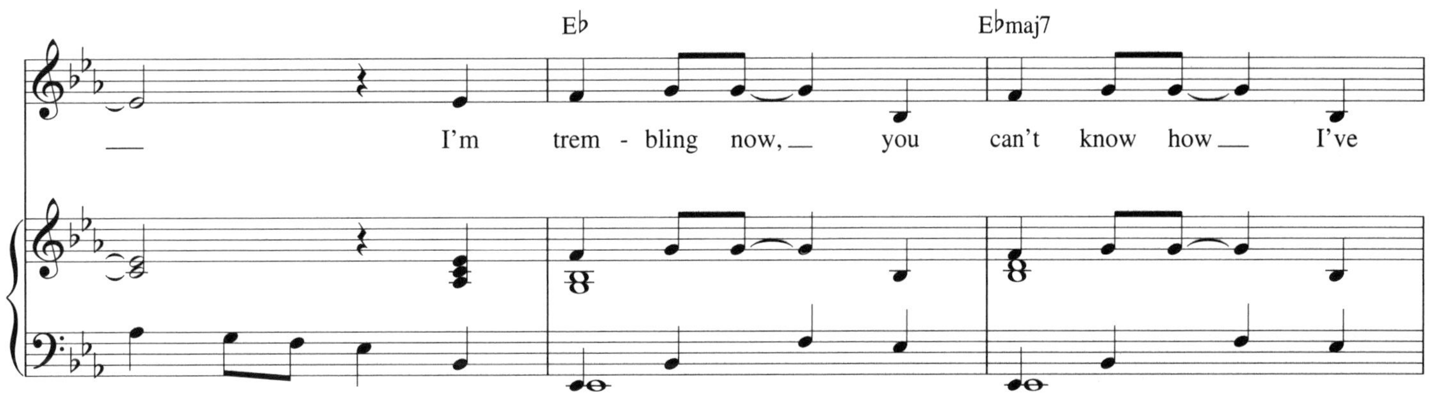

E♭
E♭maj7
I'm trem - bling now, you can't know how I've

D♭maj7
A♭/C
missed you, missed the fair - y tale ad - ven - tures

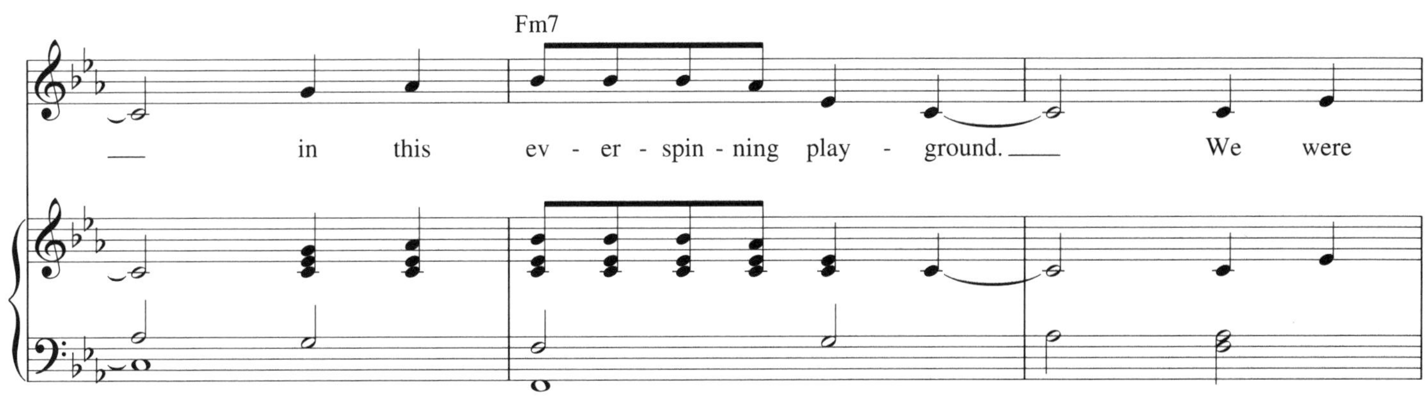

Fm7
in this ev - er - spin - ning play - ground. We were

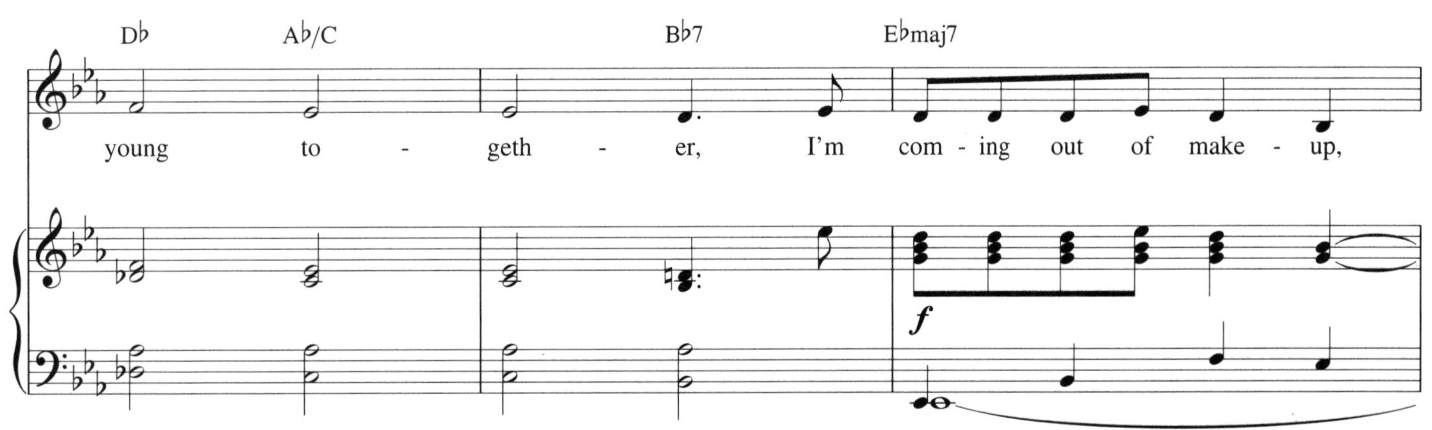

D♭
A♭/C
B♭7
E♭maj7
young to - geth - er, I'm com - ing out of make - up,
f

A♭/E♭
the light's al - read - y burn - ing, not
E♭
E♭maj7
D♭maj7
long un - til the cam - eras will start turn - ing,
A♭/C
and the ear - ly morn - ing mad - ness, and the
Fm7
E♭maj7/B♭
mag - ic in the mak - ing, yes, ev - 'ry - thing's as if we

Fm7/B♭
E♭
nev - er said good - bye.
molto accel.
Gm7
Cm7
Gm7
I don't want to be a - lone, that's all in the
Cm7
B♭
Cm
past. This world's wait - ed long e - nough,
Gm
Cm
B♭7
E♭maj7
I've come home at last, and this time will be big - ger,
f assai

A♭/E♭
and bright - er than we knew it. So
E♭
E♭maj7
D♭maj7
watch me fly, we all know I can do it.
A♭/C
Could I stop my hand from shak - ing? Has there
Fm7
D♭
A♭/C
ev - er been a mo - ment with so much to

Bb7
Ebmaj7
live for? The whis-pered con-ver-sa-tions in
p
Fm/Eb
Eb
o-ver-crowd-ed hall-ways, so much to say, not
Ebmaj7
Dbmaj7
just to-day, but al-ways. We'll have
Ab/C
Fm7
ear-ly morn-ing mad-ness, we'll have mag-ic in the mak-ing,
f

E♭maj7/B♭
A♭6/B♭
B7
yes, ev - 'ry - thing's as if we nev - er said good -
Cm
Cm/A
E♭maj7/B♭
bye,
yes, ev - 'ry - thing's as if we
A♭6/B♭
B♭7
E♭
D♭/E♭
A♭
B♭sus
nev - er said good - bye.
We taught the
3
mp
E♭
B♭
A♭/E♭
E♭
world new ways to dream.
3
f

THE BEAUTY IS
from *The Light in the Piazza*

Words and Music by
ADAM GUETTEL

It's the land of na - ked mar - ble boys!
Some - thing we don't see a lot in Win - ston Sa - lem.
That's the land of cor - du - roys!
Poco più mosso, flowing, but exact tempo
I'm just a some-one in an
mf

old mu - se - um. Far a - way from home as some-one can go.
And the beau - ty is I still meet peo - ple I know. Hel -
Expressively
lo. This is want - ing some - thing. This is reach - ing for it.
mp
This is wish - ing that a mo - ment would ar - rive. This is tak - ing chanc - es.

This is al-most touch-ing.
What the beau-ty is...
I don't un-der-stand a word they're say-ing.
I'm as dif-f'rent here as
dif-f'rent can be,
but the beau-ty is I still meet peo-ple like me.
Tempo I
Ev-ery-one's a moth-er here
poco rall.

in It - a - ly.
Ev - ery-one's a fa - ther or
sim.
a son.
I think if I had a child
poco cresc.
I would take such care of her.
Then I would - n't
feel like one.
I've

hard-ly met a sin-gle soul, but I am not a-lone. I feel
p
accel. poco a poco
Tempo II (Poco più mosso)
known! This is want-ing some-thing. This is pray-ing for it.
f
This is hold-ing breath and keep-ing fin-gers crossed. This is count-ing bless-ings.
This is won-d'ring when I'll see that boy a-gain.

I've got a feel - ing he's just a some - one
too.
pp
And the beau - ty is when you re - al - ize,
cresc.
rall. poco a poco
mf
Broader
when you re - al - ize some - one could be look - ing for a some - one like
sfz
8vb
Più mosso
you.
mf
rit.

A CHANGE IN ME

from Walt Disney's *Beauty and the Beast: The Broadway Musical*

Words by TIM RICE
Music by ALAN MENKEN

* *Original Broadway key: G♭*

C♯
F♯m
F♯m/E
D
A/C♯
that good can come from bad. That may not make me wise
Bm
E7sus
E
A
Bm7
but oh, it makes me glad. And I,
A/C♯
D
Esus
E
A
Bm7
A/C♯
I nev - er thought I'd leave be - hind
Bm/D
Bm
Esus
E
A
Bm7
my child - hood dreams, but I don't mind,

A/C♯
D
E7
F♯m
C♯m/E
For now I love the world I see.
Bm/D
F♯/C♯
Bm7
E7
A
D
E
No change of heart, a change in me.
A
D
E7
A
D
Esus
E
For in my dark de-spair
A
D
Esus
E
A/C♯
F♯m
A/C♯
I slow - ly un - der-stood.
My per - fect world out there

Bm/D
A/E
E7
C
F
Gsus
G
had dis - ap - peared for good,
But in its place I feel
E
Am
Am/G
F
C/E
a tru - er life be-gin.
And it's so good and real,
L.H.
Dm7
G
C
Dm7
It must come from with-in. And I,
poco rall.
mf
a tempo
C/E
F
F/G
C
I nev - er thought I'd leave be - hind

Dm7
C/E
Fmaj7
F6
Dm7
G7sus
G
my child - hood dreams, but I don't
C
Dm7
C/E
mind.
I'm where and
F
F/G
Am
Am/G
who I want to be.
Dm/F
A/E
Dm7
G7sus
G7
C
No change of heart, a change in me.
mp

F
G
C
F
Gsus
G
Am
Dm7
G7sus
G7
No change of heart, a change in
p
C
F
G
C
me.
F
G
C

CHRISTMAS LULLABY

from *Songs for a New World*

Music and Lyrics by
JASON ROBERT BROWN

C
Dm7
3
F5/C
F5/B♭
never be the kind who simply waves her hand and
Dm7
C(add2)/E
F
F5/G
C
mp
G/B
has a mil - lion peo - ple do the things I wish I'd done. But in the eyes
legato
mp poco accel.
Warmly, poco rubato
Am
Em/G
F
C/E
Dsus
D
of Heav - en, my place is as - sured. I
C/G
Am7(add4)
Dsus
D
Gmaj9
E/G♯
car - ry with me Heav - en's grand de - sign.

Am
C/G
F
C/E
D7
p
"Glo - ri - a! Glo - ri - a!" I will sing the name of the Lord, and He will
F5(add2)
C/E
D7sus
C/F
C/E
Dm7
mp G7sus
make me shine... And I will be
p
mp
Steadily
C
Dm7(add4)
C(add9)/E
B♭
like Moth-er Mar - y with a bless-ing in my soul, and I will
Am7
G5(add2)
F
F/G
C
give the world my eyes so they can see. And I will be like Moth-er Mar -

Dm7(add4) C(add9)/E B♭ Am7 Gsus C5/F
mp
3
-ry with a bless-ing in my soul, and the fu-ture of the world inside of me.
mp
C Dm7 F5/C F5/B♭ C(add9)
bring out; lyrically
Dm7 F(add9) G7sus E/G♯ Am(add2) Em/G
mf
In the eyes of Heav-en, my
rich and warm
mf
F C/E Dsus D C(add2)/G Am7sus Am
place is as-sured. I car-ry with me Heav-en's grand de-sign.

Dsus
D
Gmaj9
E/G#
Am
C(add2)/G
"Glo - ri - a! Glo - ri - a!" I will
C5/F
C/E
D7(add4)
C5/F
C/E
D7sus
C/F
C/E
Dm7
sing the name of the Lord, and He will make me shine.
colla voce
F/G
G7sus
C
Dm7(add4)
C/E
And I will be like Moth-er Mar - y with a bless-ing in my soul,
poco allarg.
more steadily
B♭
Am7
G5(add2)
F
and I will give the world my eyes so they can see.

G5
C
Dm7(add4)
C/E
And I will be like Moth-er Mar - y with a bless-ing in my soul,
Bb
Am7(add4)
Gsus
C5/F
F/G
C5(add9)
and the fu - ture of the world in - side of me.
mf
f poco accel.
F5/G
C
Dm7
C/E
And I will be like Moth-er Mar - y with the pow-er in my veins
with passion
F5/Bb
Am7
C5/G
F
to be - lieve in all the things I've yet to be!

C
Dm7
C/E
B♭(add2)/D
And I will be like Moth-er Mar - y and I'll suf-fer an - y pains...
Rubato
p
Am7
Gsus
C5/F
Am7
Gsus
For the fu - ture of the world...
(simply; poco accel.)
C5/F
Am7(add4)
Gsus
C5/F
G7sus
For the fu - ture of the world, in - side of me.
slowly, deliberately
mp
C
Dm7
F5/B♭
C5
Come prima
p
(roll slowly)

COME TO YOUR SENSES

from *tick, tick... BOOM!*

Words and Music by
JONATHAN LARSON

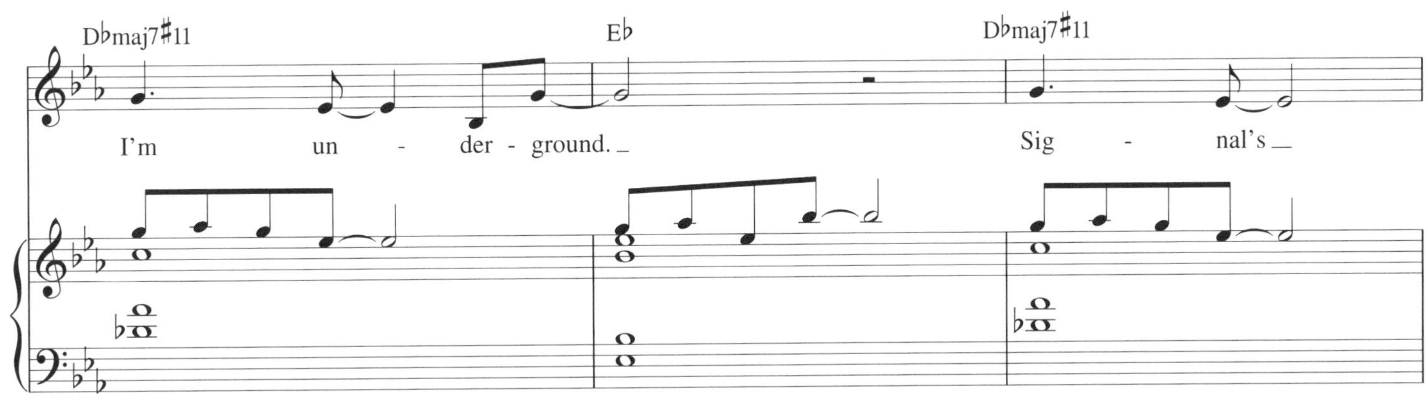

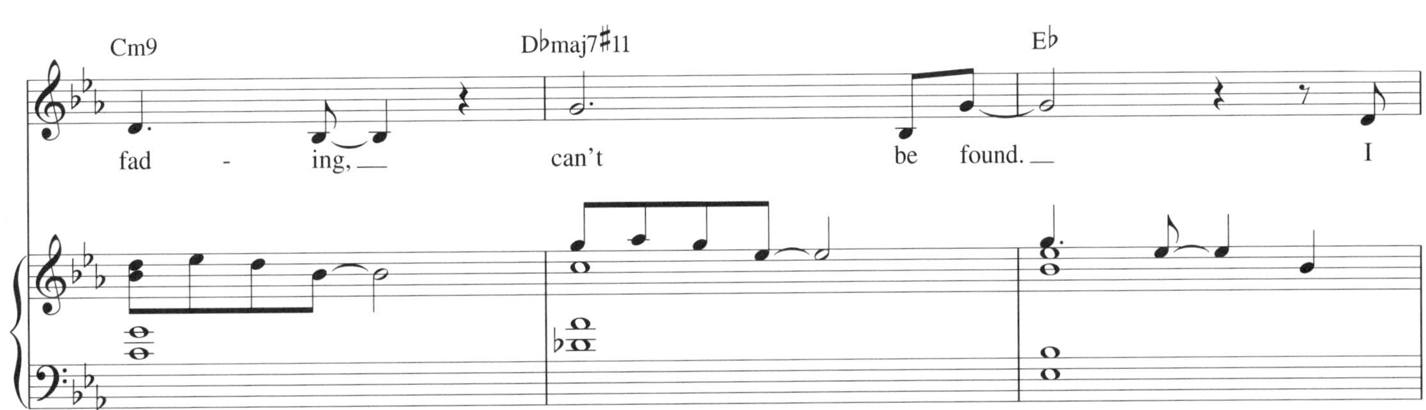

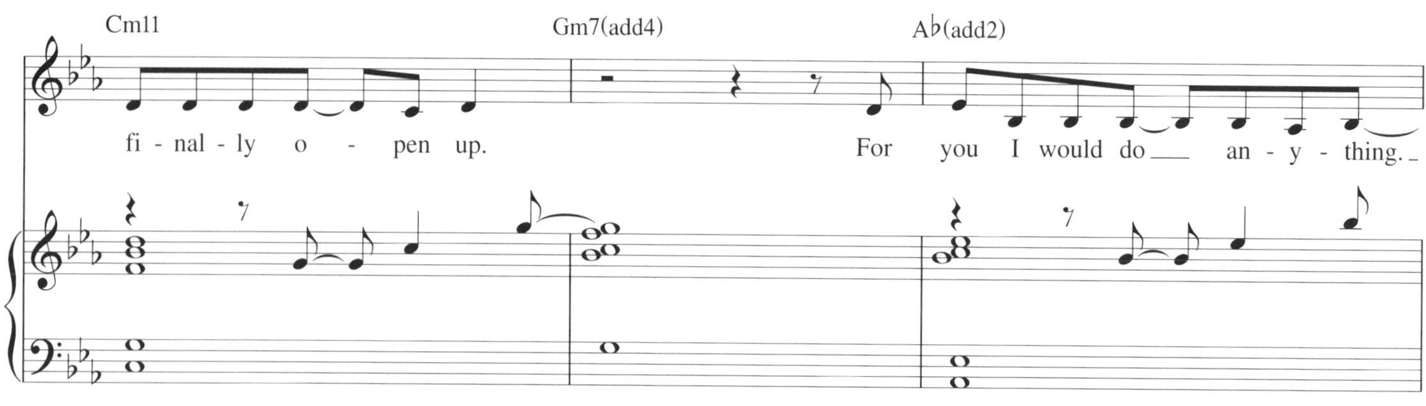
Cm11
Gm7(add4)
A♭(add2)
fi - nal - ly o - pen up.
For you I would do anything.

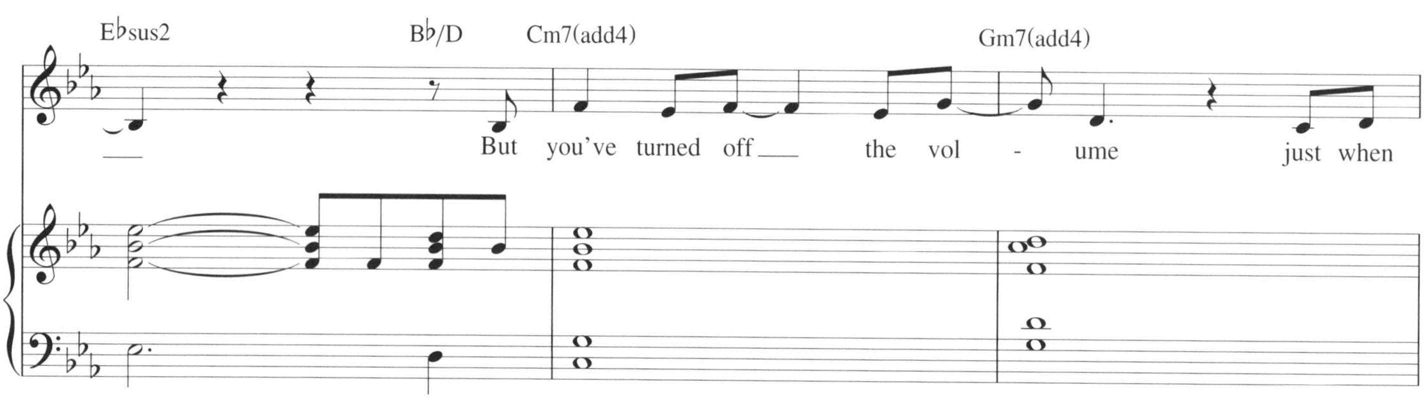
E♭sus2
B♭/D
Cm7(add4)
Gm7(add4)
But you've turned off the vol - ume just when

A♭(add2)
B♭sus
B♭
I've be - gun to sing.

E♭sus2
Gm7
A♭(add2)
Come to your sens - es. De - fens - es are not the way to go, and you know, or at least
mp

Cm7
Bbsus
Ebsus2
Gm7
you knew.
Ev-'ry-thing's strange, you've changed, and I don't know what to do
Ab(add2)
Cm7
Bb
Abmaj7
Gbmaj7
to get through. I don't know what to do.
Eb/Db
Cm9
I have to laugh, we
Eb/Db
Eb
Eb/Db
sure put on a show.
Love is pas-sé in

Cm9
Eb/Db
Eb
this day and age. How can we ex - pect it to grow?

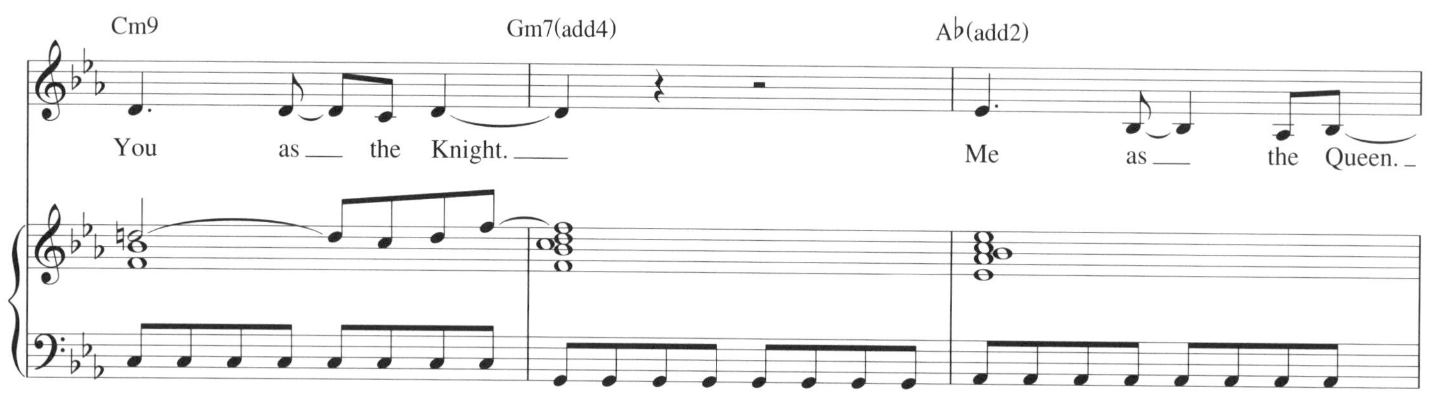
Cm9
Gm7(add4)
Ab(add2)
You as the Knight. Me as the Queen.

Ebsus
Bb/D
Cm7(add4)
Gm7(add4)
All I've got to - night is

Ab(add2)
Bbsus
Bb
stat - ic on a screen.

E♭sus2
Gm7
A♭maj9
Come to your sens - es. The fenc - es in - side are not for real if we feel as we did,
mf a little detached

Cm7
B♭sus
B♭
E♭sus2
Gm7
and I do. Can't you re - call when this all be - gan? It was on - ly

A♭maj9
Cm7
B♭sus
E♭(add2)
you and me. It was on - ly me and you.

C♭(add2)
D♭(add2)
But now the air is filled with con -
f

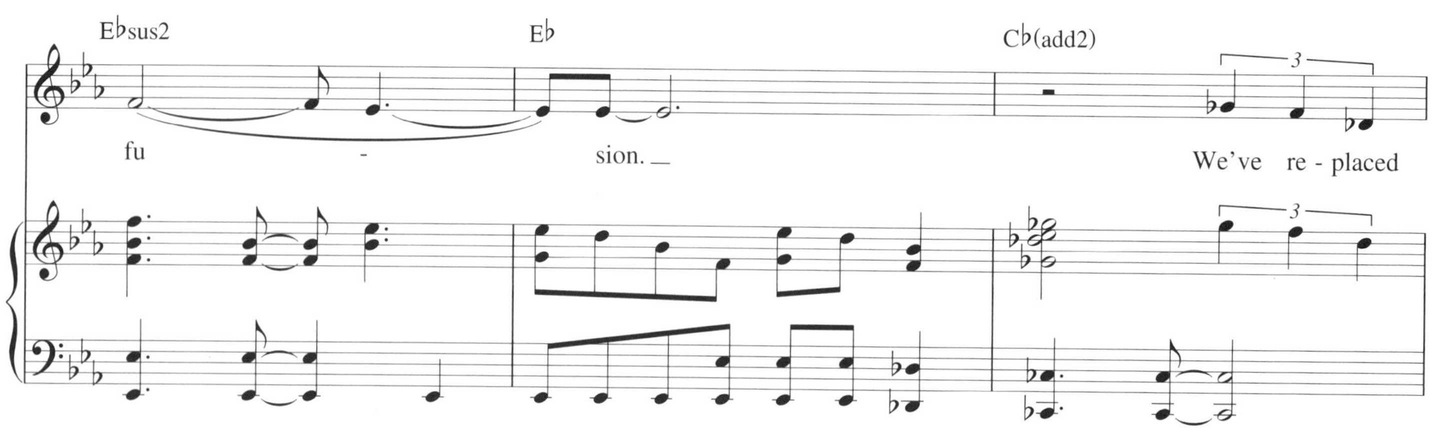
E♭sus2
E♭
C♭(add2)
fu - sion.
We've re - placed

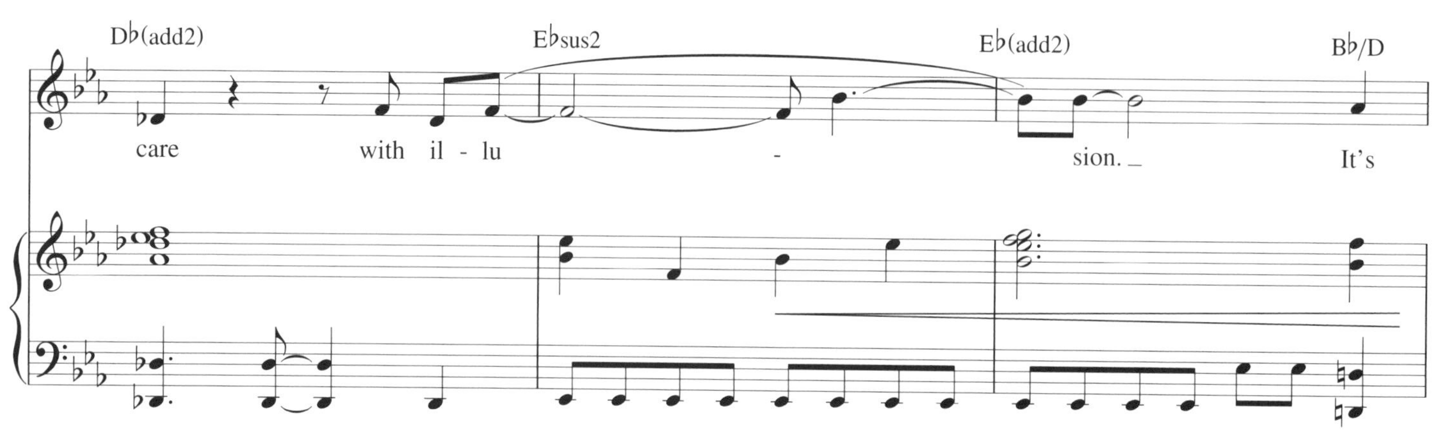
D♭(add2)
E♭sus2
E♭(add2)
B♭/D
care with il - lu - sion.
It's

Cm9
Gm7(add4)
A♭sus2
cool to be cold.
Noth-ing lasts an - y - more.
sub. mp

E♭sus2
B♭/D
Cm9
Gm7(add4)
Love be - comes dis - pos - a - ble. This is the shape

Majestically

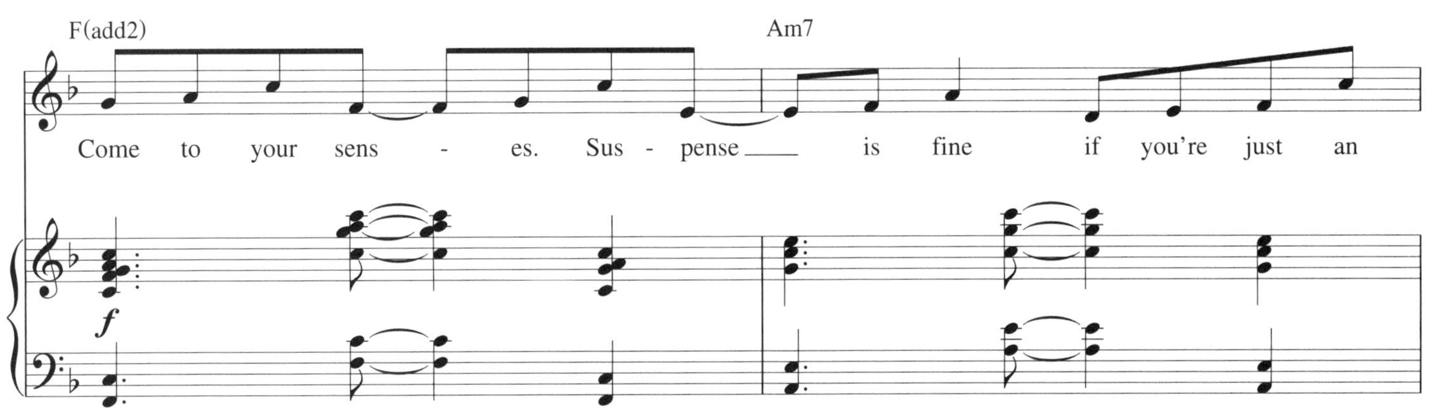

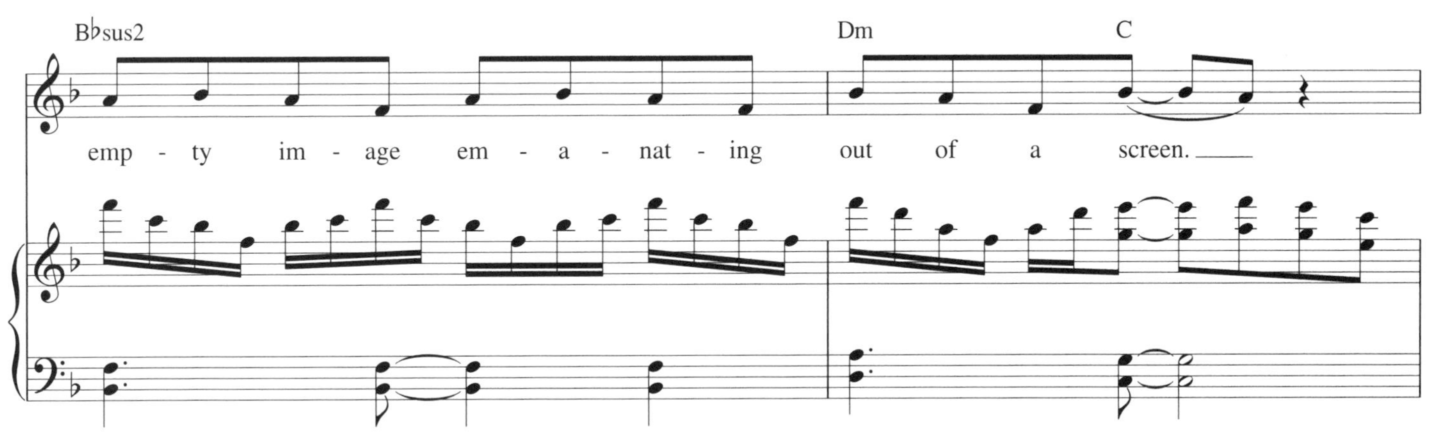

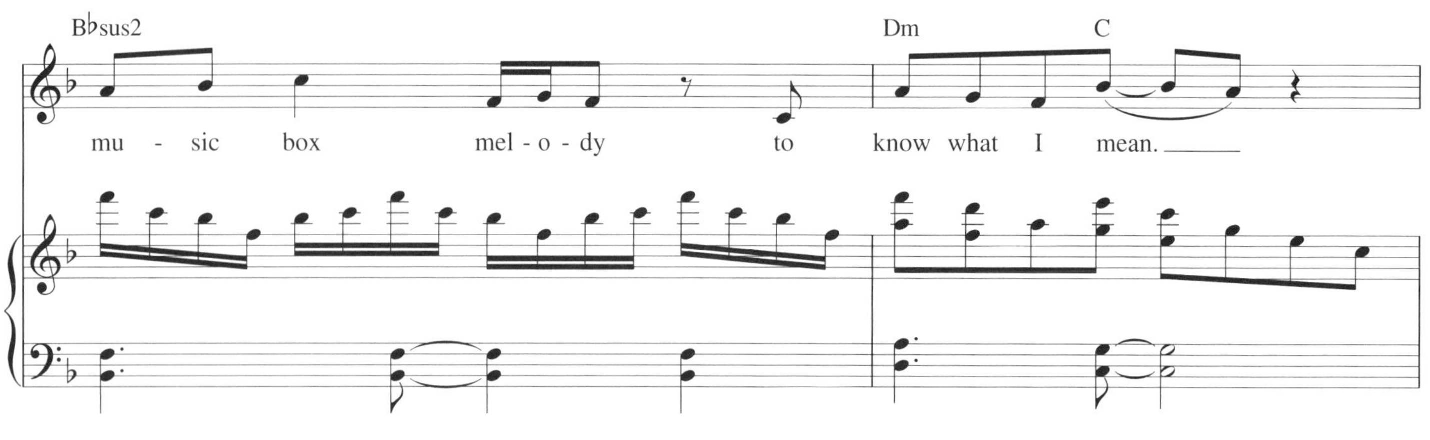

B♭sus2
Dm
C
mu - sic box mel - o - dy to know what I mean.

B♭sus2
F/A
B♭sus2
Deep in my eyes, what do you see? Deep in my sighs,

Dm
B♭sus2
F/A
lis - ten to me. Let the mu - sic com - mence from in - side.

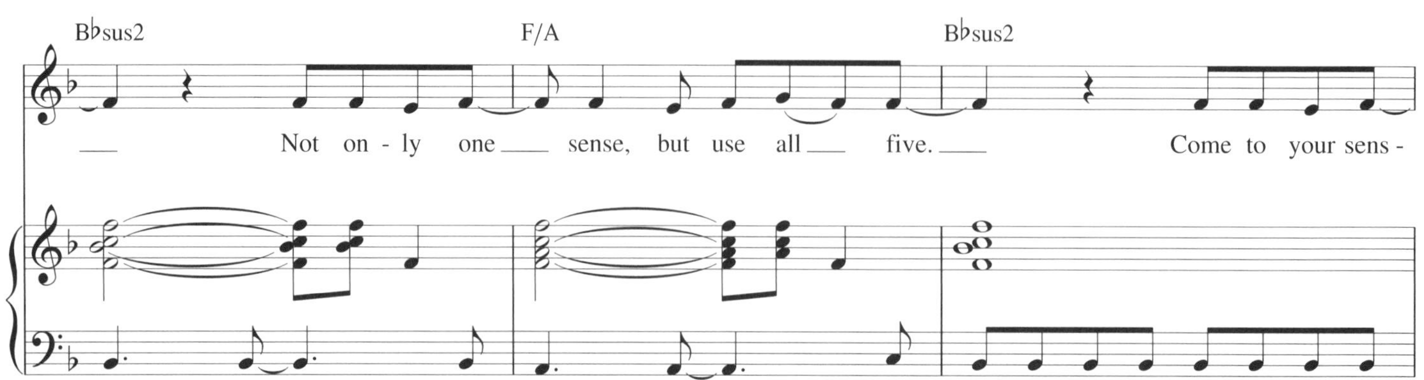

B♭sus2
F/A
B♭sus2
Not on - ly one sense, but use all five. Come to your sens -

F/A
B♭sus2
F/A
- es.
Come to your sens - es.

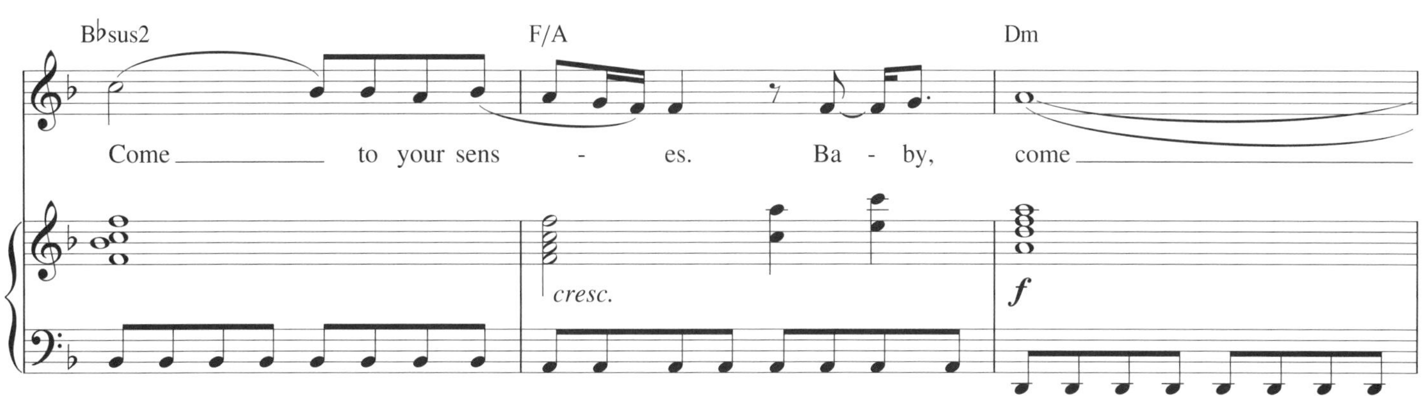
B♭sus2
F/A
Dm
Come to your sens - es. Ba - by, come
cresc.
f

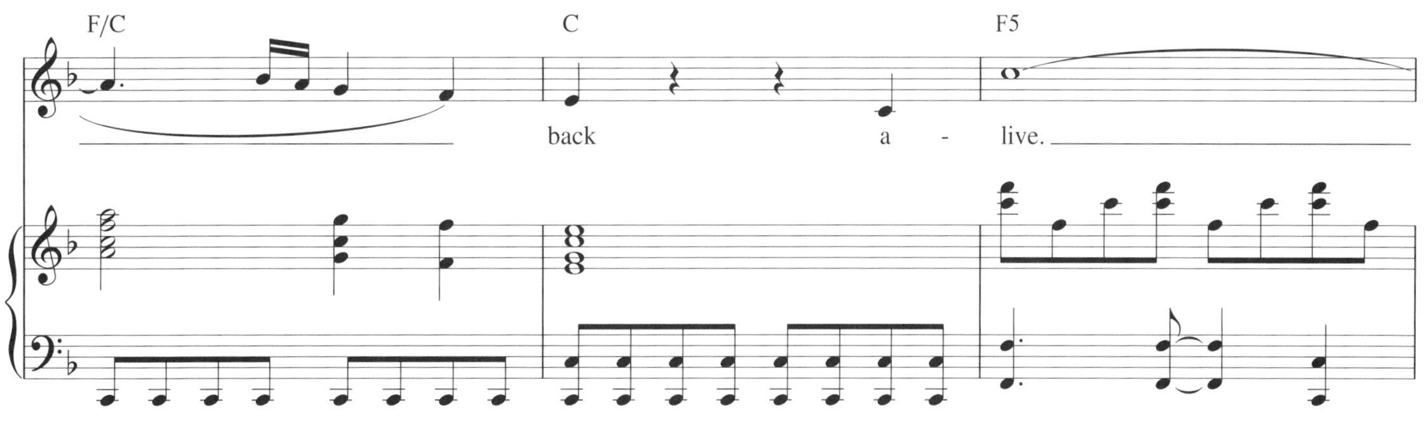
F/C
C
F5
back a - live.

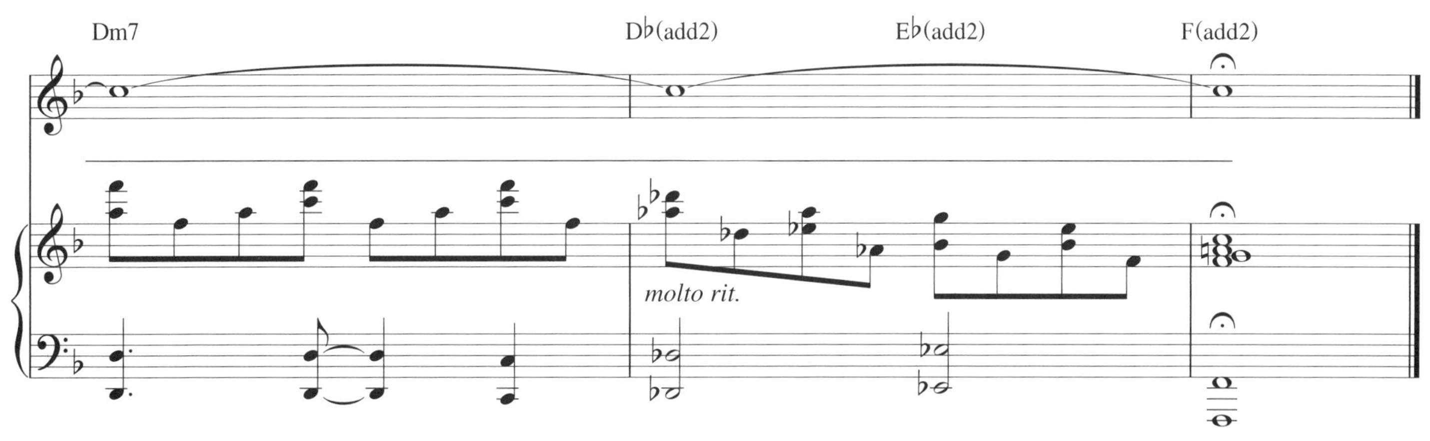
Dm7
D♭(add2)
E♭(add2)
F(add2)
molto rit.

THE DARK I KNOW WELL

from *Spring Awakening*

Music by DUNCAN SHEIK
Lyrics by STEVEN SATER

Sung by various characters (as indicated), the song can be sung as a solo.

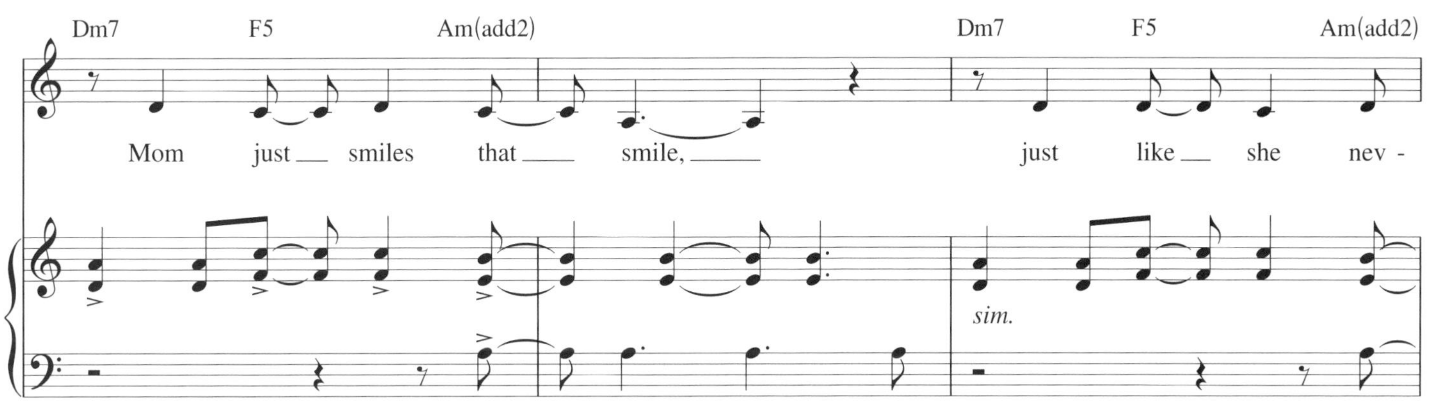
Dm7
F5
Am(add2)
Dm7
F5
Am(add2)
Mom just smiles that smile, just like she nev -
sim.

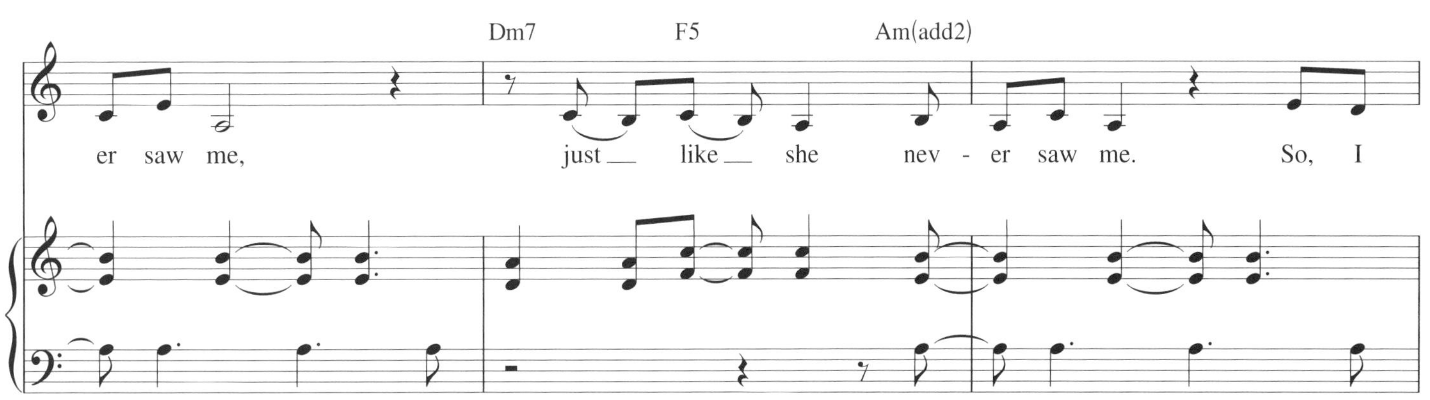
Dm7
F5
Am(add2)
er saw me, just like she nev - er saw me. So, I

Dm7
F5
Am(add2)
Dm7
F5
Am(add2)
leave, want - in' just to hide, know - in' deep in - side

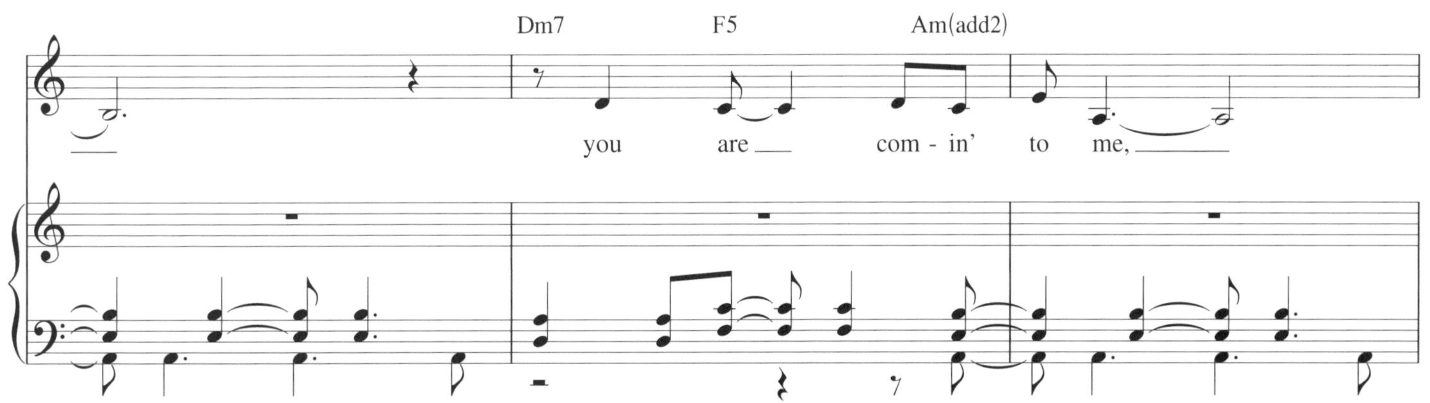
Dm7
F5
Am(add2)
you are com - in' to me,

Dm7
F5
Am(add2)
E(add♭6)
you are com - in' to me... You say all you want is just a kiss
MORITZ, OTTO,
GEORG, MALE ENSEMBLE:
(2nd time only) Ah
Am(add2)
good - night, then you hold me and you whis - per, "Child, the Lord won't mind. It's just you
ah
Gsus
F
and me. Child, you're a beau - ty.
Child, you're a beau - ty.

E(add♭6)
God, it's good— the lov - in'. Ain't it good to - night? You ain't
Ah
ff

Am(add2)
Gsus
seen noth-in' yet— gon - na { treat / teach } you right. It's just you and me.
ah

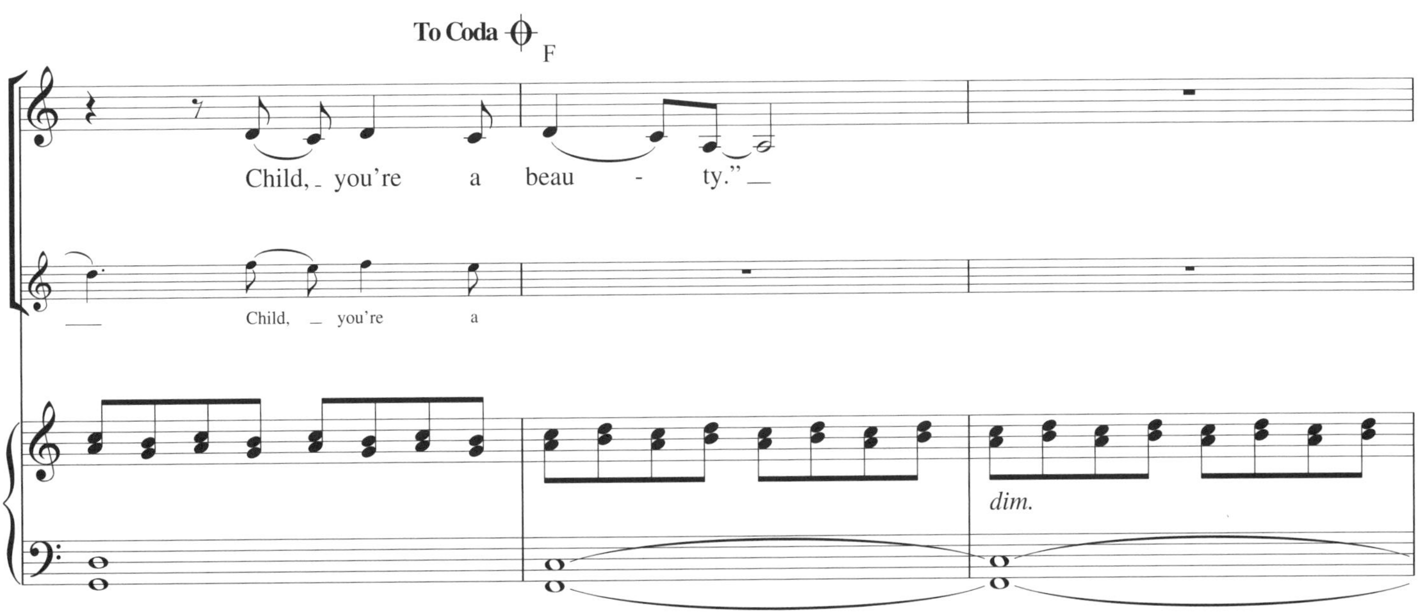
To Coda
F
Child, you're a beau - ty."
Child, you're a
dim.

ILSE:
Dm7 F5 Am(add2)
I don't scream, though I know it's wrong.
mp
Dm7 F5 Am(add2)
I just play a - long.
Dm7 F5 Am(add2)
I lie there and breathe,
Dm7 F5 Am(add2)
lie there and breathe. I wan - na be
Dm7 F5 Am(add2)
strong, I want the world to find out
Dm7 F5 Am(add2)
that you're dream - in' on

Dm7
F5
Am(add2)
me,
me and my "beau - ty,"

Dm7
F5
Am(add2)
add MARTHA:
D.S. al Coda
me and my "beau - ty."
You say all

CODA

F
Add first ENSEMBLE GIRL:
E(addb6)
beau - ty."
There is a part I can't tell
beau - ty.
Ah,
f

Am(add2)
'bout the dark I know well.
dark I know well.

Add second ENSEMBLE GIRL:
Gsus
There is a part I can't tell
Ah

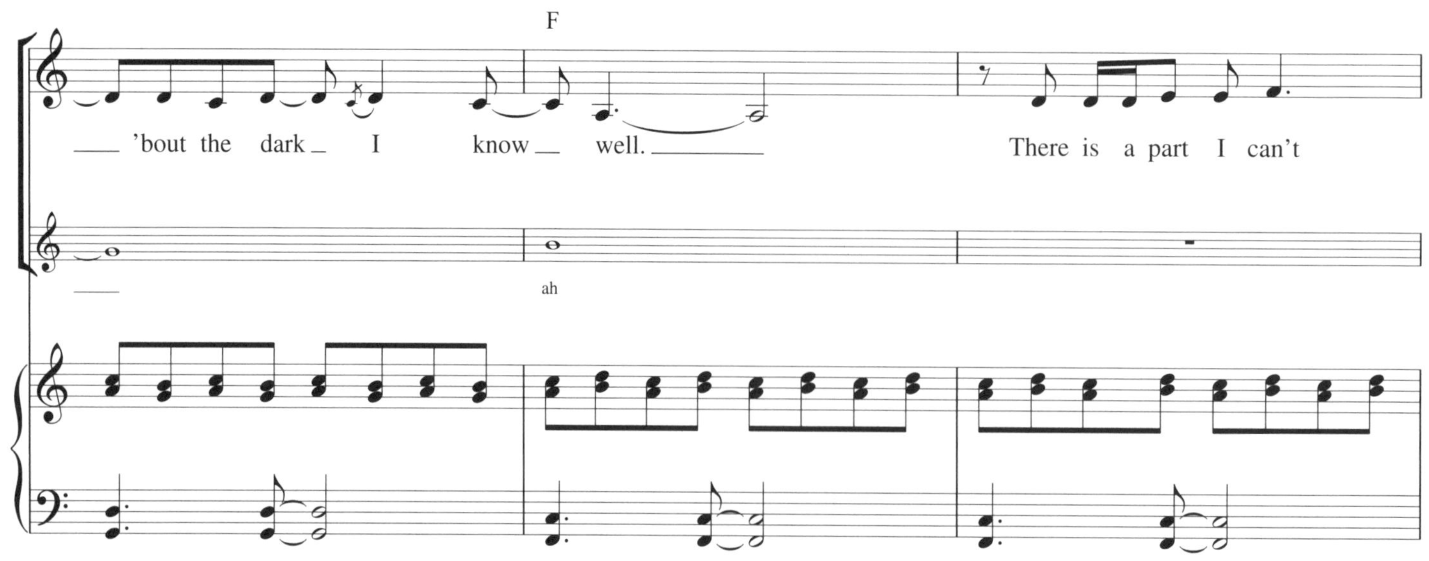
F
'bout the dark I know well.
There is a part I can't
ah

E(add♭6)
Am(add2)
tell ’bout the dark I know well.
ah, dark I know well.

Gsus
There is a part I can’t tell
Ah

F
’bout the dark I know well.
ah.

DEFYING GRAVITY
from the Broadway Musical *Wicked*

Music and Lyrics by
STEPHEN SCHWARTZ

D♭
C♭sus2
D♭sus
D♭
- ond guess - ing,
too late to go back to sleep
G♭5/E♭
G♭5/F
D♭/G♭
It's time to trust my in - stincts,
close my eyes and
Allegro
A♭sus
A♭
B♭m7(no5th)
G♭sus2
leap...
It's time to try de - fy -
8va
With pedal
A♭sus
- ing grav - i - ty
I think I'll

Bbm7(no5th) Gbsus2 Absus
try de-fy - ing grav - i - ty, and you can't pull me down.
cresc.
Db5 Ab/Eb Db/F Gbsus2 Db5 Ab/Eb Db/F Gbsus2
mf
Db5 Ab/Eb Db/F Gbsus2 Ab(add4) Db5 Ab/Eb Db/F Gbsus2
I'm through ac - cept - ing lim - its 'cause some-one says
Dbsus2 Db5 Ab/Eb Db/F Gbsus2 Ab(add4) Db/F
they're so. Some things I can - not change, but 'til

G♭sus2
C♭sus2
D♭5
I try, I'll nev - er know
Too long I've been
D♭sus
D♭
C♭sus2
D♭5
a - fraid of los - ing love I guess I've lost
G♭5/E♭
G♭5/F
D♭/G♭
A♭sus
Well, if that's love, it comes at much too high a cost...
A♭
B♭m7(no5th)
G♭sus2
A♭sus
I'd soon - er buy de - fy - ing
8va

B♭m7(no5th)
G♭sus2
grav - i - ty Kiss me good - bye, I'm de - fy -
A♭sus
A♭7sus
- ing grav - i - ty, and you can't pull me
Moderato, dreamily
Amaj9♯11
down.
Un - lim - it - ed...
B6(add4)
My fu - ture is
p

C♯m9
Amaj9♯11
B6(add4)
Emaj7
un - lim - it - ed.
And I've just had a
Amaj9♯11
G♯m11
C♯m11
Bsus/A
Am6
vi - sion al - most like a proph - e - cy,
I know–
mf
rit.
Freely
E/G♯
A(add9)
E/B
B9sus
G(add9)
Gmaj7
G6
It sounds tru - ly cra - zy, and true, the vi - sion's ha - zy...
But I swear some - day I'll
p
Allegro; as before
Cmaj9
C6
Cmaj7
G♯m7(no5th)
Esus2
F♯sus
be up in the sky, de - fy - ing
mf

G♯m7(no5th)
E sus2
grav - i - ty
Fly - ing so high,
de - fy -
F♯sus
F♯7sus
- ing
grav - i - ty,
They'll
nev - er
pull me
down...
B 5
F♯/C♯ B/D♯
E sus2
D♭5
A♭/E♭
D♭/F
G♭sus2
Triumphantly
D♭5
G♭sus2
So if you care
f

D♭5
G♭sus2
A♭
to find me,
look to the west - ern sky
D♭5
A♭/E♭
D♭/F
G♭sus2
A♭(add4)
E♭m/G♭
E♭m
As some-one told me late - ly: ev - 'ry - one de-serves
rall.
D♭/F
D♭
C♭sus2
D♭5
D♭sus
D♭
the chance to fly! And if I'm fly - ing so - lo,
a tempo
C♭sus2
D♭5
G♭5/E♭
at least I'm fly - ing free
To those who'd ground

G♭5/F
D♭/G♭
A♭sus
me, take a mes - sage back from me…
A♭
B♭m7(no5th)
G♭sus2
A♭sus
Tell them how I am de - fy - ing
8va
grav - i - ty I'm fly - ing high de - fy -
B♭m7(no5th)
G♭sus2
A♭sus
E♭m/F
Fm7
- ing grav - i - ty, and soon I'll match them in re -
rall.

With determination
B♭m
G♭m/A
A♭sus/G♭
nown...
And no - bod - y in
sub. p
A♭7sus/F
A♭m7/E♭
A♭m7(add4)/E♭
A♭9sus/D♭
G♭(add9)/D♭
all of Oz, no Wiz - ard that there is or was is
G♭m(add9)/A
E♭m7♭5/G♭
A♭sus
A♭7sus
D♭5
A♭(add4)/E♭
D♭/F
G♭sus2
D♭/F
ev - er gon - na bring me down...
rall.
ff
rall.
C♭(add2)/B♭
G♭/C♭
D♭
Ah!

DON'T CRY OUT LOUD

(We Don't Cry Out Loud)

from *The Boy from Oz*

Words and Music by
PETER ALLEN and CAROLE BAYER SAGER

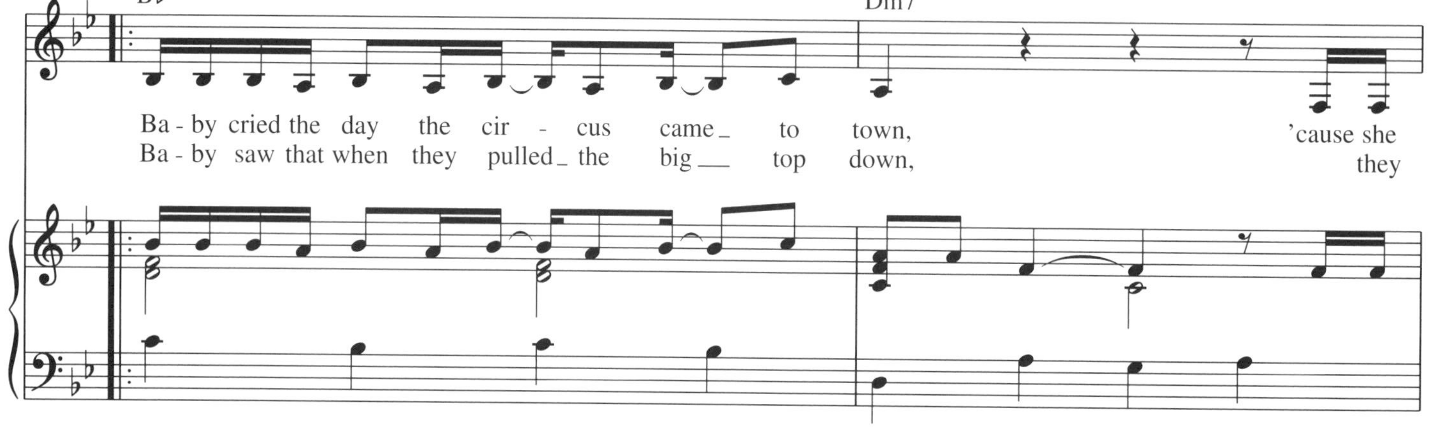

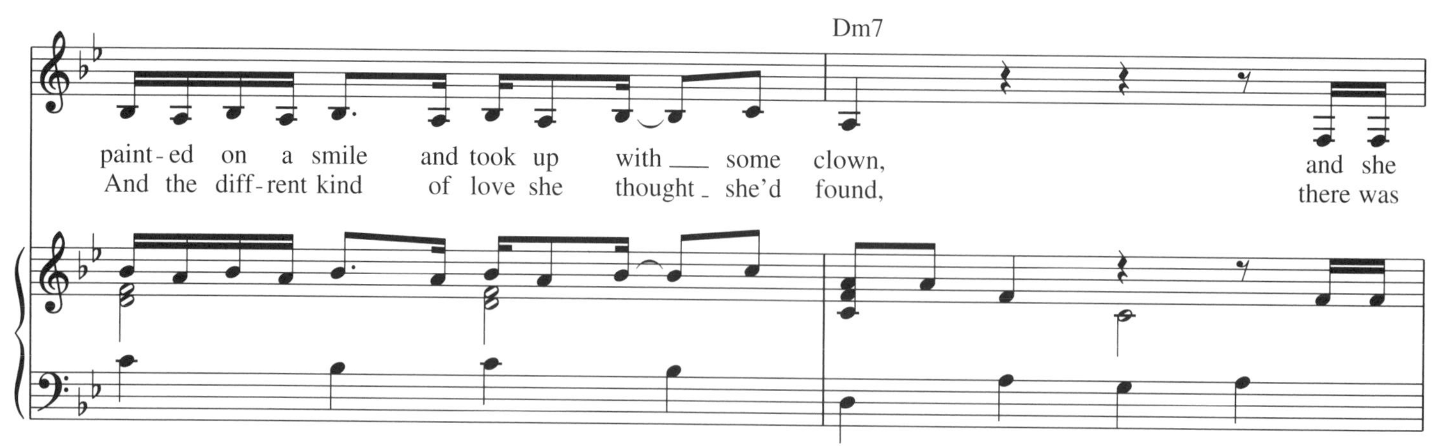

Cm7 F11 Bb F/A
danced with-out a net up on the wire. I
noth-ing more than saw-dust and some glit-ter. But
Gm Dm
know a-lot a-bout her 'cause you see,
ba-by can't be bro-ken 'cause you see, she
Gm C7 F7sus F7
ba-by is an aw-ful lot like me.
had the fin-est teach-er, that was me. I taught her:
Bb F/A Gm Cm Eb+/B
Don't cry out loud, just keep it in-side learn how to

Cm/B♭
F11
F
B♭
F/A
Gm
hide your feel-ings.
Fly high and proud
and if you should
Cm
E♭+/B
fall
re-mem-ber you
1
Cm/B♭
F11
Gmaj7
al-most had it all.
Cm7
Dm7
Cm7/E♭
F11
2
Cm7/B♭
F11
al-most had it all
Gm
F♯7sus

B
F♯/A♯
G♯m
C♯m
E+/B♯
Don't cry out loud, just keep it in - side, learn how to
Fly high and proud, and if you should fall re-mem-ber you
f

1
2
E/B
F♯11
F♯
C♯m/B
E/F♯
F♯
B
hide your feel - ings.
al - most had it all.

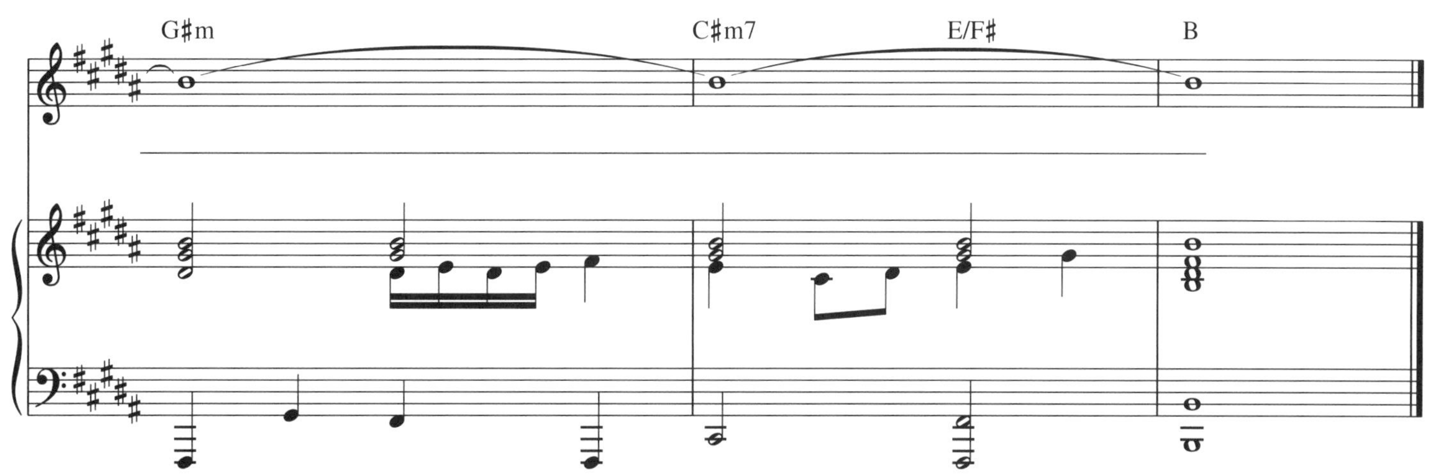
G♯m
C♯m7
E/F♯
B

EASY AS LIFE

from Elton John and Tim Rice's *Aida*

Music by ELTON JOHN
Lyrics by TIM RICE

Slow

Ab G Ab G7 Cm(add4) Cm

This is the mo-ment when the Gods ex-pect me to beg for help. But I won't

mp *colla voce*

Eb/Bb Fm6/Ab Fm7/Ab Gsus G

e - ven try. I want noth-ing in the world but my - self to pro-tect me. And I

Fm7 Gsus G

won't lie down, roll o - ver and die.

Flowing

Cm

mp

Cm7 Fm/C Cm Cm7 Fm/C

Cm
All I have to do is for-get how much I love him.
A♭maj7
A♭6
B♭(add9)
All I have to do is put my long-ing to one
Cm
side.
Cm/B♭
Tell my - self that love's
an ev - er-chang - ing sit - u - a - tion.
F(add9)/A
F/A

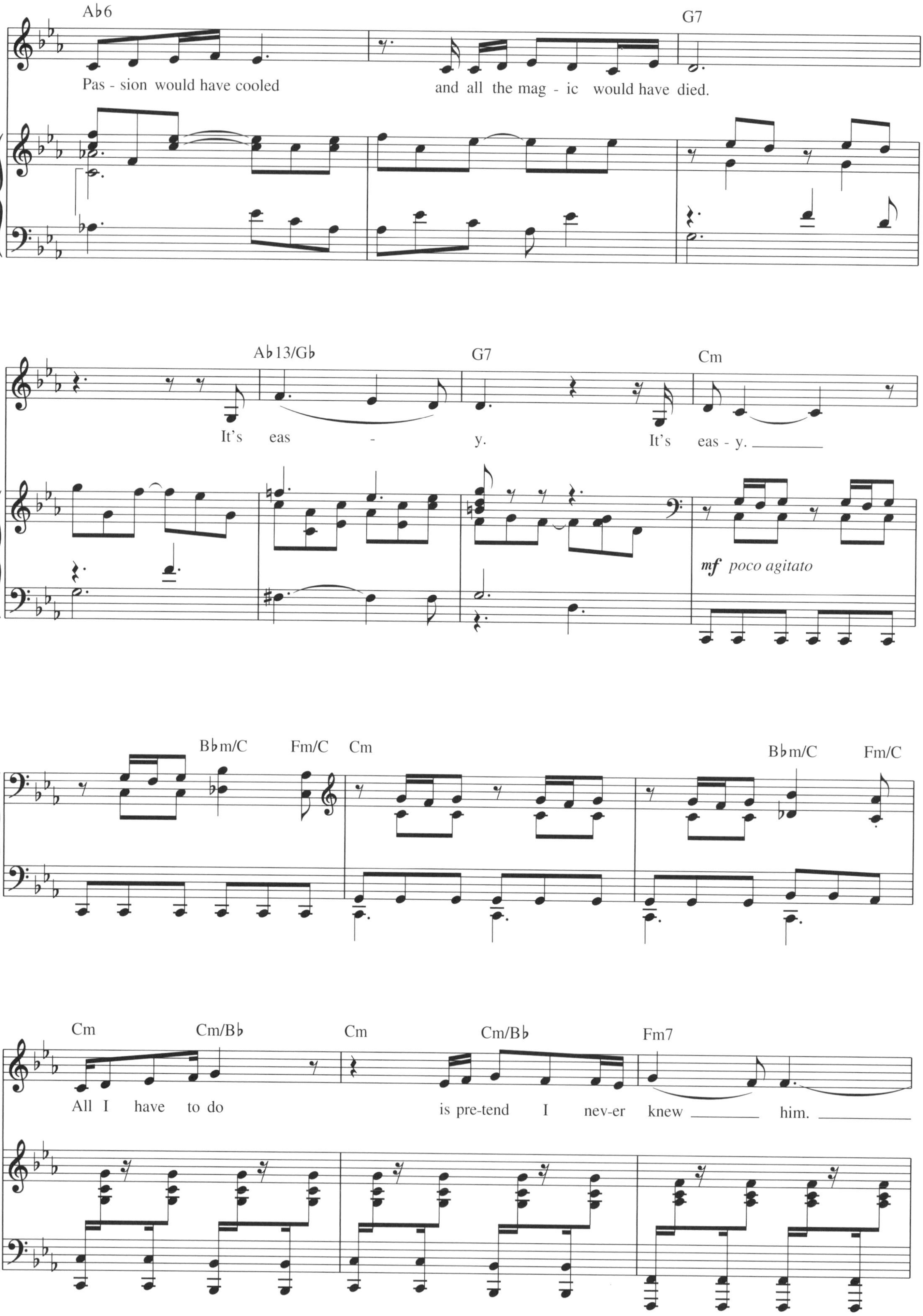

A♭6 G7

Pas - sion would have cooled and all the mag - ic would have died.

A♭13/G♭ G7 Cm

It's eas - y. It's eas - y. ____

mf poco agitato

B♭m/C Fm/C Cm B♭m/C Fm/C

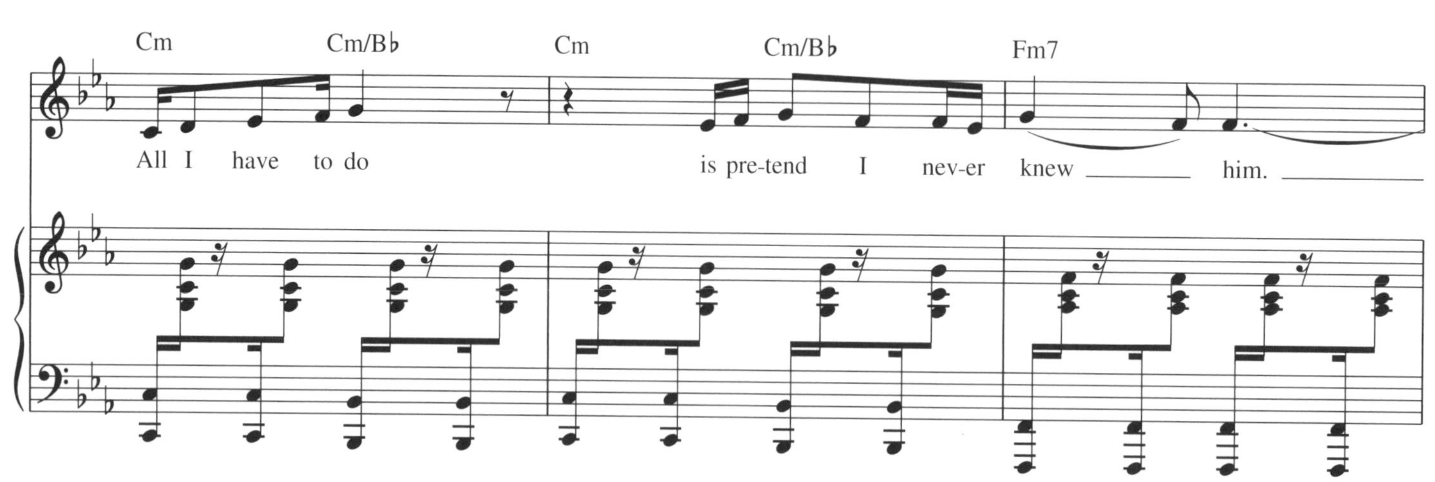

B♭(add9)
On those ver - y rare oc - ca - sions when he steals in - to my
Cm
heart
Cm/B♭
bet - ter to have lost him
when the ties were bare - ly bind - ing.
F(add9)/A
mf
A♭6
Bet - ter the con - tempt of the fa - mil - iar can - not start.
Gsus
cresc.

G7
Ab13/Gb
G7
It's eas - y. It's
Cm7
Bbm/C
Fm/C
Fm7/Ab
eas - y.
Un - til I think a-bout him
f
mf
G7sus
G7
as he was when I last touched him and
Fm7/Ab
G7sus
G7
how he would have been were I to be with him to - day.
mf

Bbm7/Db
Those ver - y rare oc-cas - ions don't let up. They keep on
C7#5 C7 Bbm7
com - ing. All I ev-er want - ed
N.C. G/B C Ab13/Gb
and I'm throw-ing it a - way. It's eas -
G.P.
mp
mf
G7sus G7 Ab13/Gb G7
y. It's eas - y as

Cm
Ab/C Abmaj7/C
Bb
Cm
Ab6
Cm7
life.
f
Cm
Ab/C
Bb
Cm
Cm7
But then I see the fac - es
Fm7
Bb(add9)
of a worn, de-feat-ed peo - ple,
a fa-ther and a na-tion
mf
Cm7
Cm7/Bb
who won't let a cow-ard run.
Is this how the gods

Am7♭5
F/A
re-ward the faith - ful through the ag - es?
Fm/A♭
Fm(add9)/A♭
G7
Forc-ing us to prove that all the hard-est things we've done
A♭/G♭
G7
Cm
are eas - y, so easy-y.
dim.
mp
B♭m/C
Fm/C
Fm/A♭
And though I'll think a-bout him till the earth draws in a -
f

G7sus
G7
Fm/A♭
round _ me, ___ and though I choose to leave him for an-oth-er kind of
G7sus
G7
B♭m7/D♭
love, ___ this is no de - ni - al,
C7♯5
C7
B♭m7
no be-tray - al, but re- demp - tion ___ re- deemed in my own eyes
f
G/B
C
A♭13/G♭
and in the pan-the-on a - bove. ___ It's eas -
mp

G7
A♭13/G♭
G7sus
G7
Cm
y. It's eas - y as life.
f
A♭13/G♭
G7sus
G7
Cm
It's eas - y as life.
B♭m/C
Fm/C
A♭13/G♭
G7sus
G7
Cm
It's eas - y as life.
mf
ff
Broadly
A♭
A♭maj7
G7sus
Cm
molto rall.

FIND YOUR GRAIL

from *Monty Python's Spamalot*

Lyrics by ERIC IDLE
Music by JOHN DU PREZ and ERIC IDLE

This is a parody pop/rock ballad. The original cast singer imitated many clichéd styles in the song.

strong. Keep right on to the end of your song Do not
mf
fail Find your Grail Find your Grail. Find your Grail.
Life is real - ly up to you. You must choose what to pur - sue.
f
Set your mind on what to find, and there's

noth - ing you can't do.
So keep right to the
mf
end. You'll find your goal, my friend. You won't fail. Find your
Grail. Find your Grail. Find your Grail. Life is real - ly
f
up to you. You must choose what to pur - sue.

Set your mind on what to find, And there's noth-ing you can't do, you can't
from here to the end Lady of the Lake improvises as an over-the-top pop diva.
do So keep right to the
poco rall.
ff a tempo
end. You'll find your goal, my friend. You won't fail. Find your
Grail. Find your Grail. Find your Grail.
rall.

THE FLAGMAKER, 1775

from *Songs for a New World*

Music and Lyrics by
JASON ROBERT BROWN

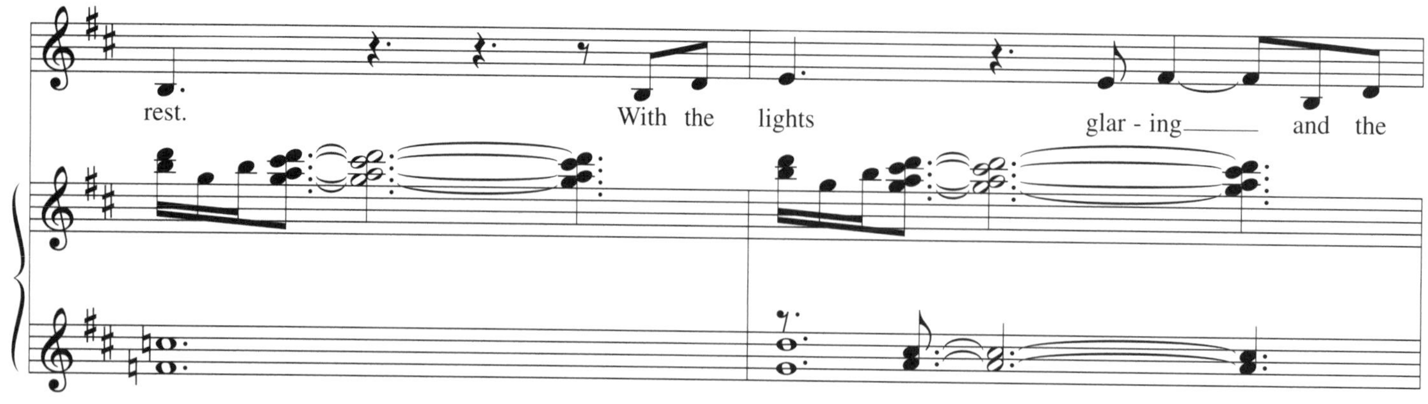

calls sound - ing and the clench - ing in your
chest…
When the man's in bat - tle, and the
mf
ba - by's rat - tle on - ly makes you more de - pressed, the
wise wo - man does what she knows:
If it's fight - ing, she fights; if it's sew - ing, she sews. When the
p colla voce, rubato

In Tempo
ten-sion in-side o-ver-flows and goes too far, one more
mp
star, one more stripe, to es-cape your lone-ly bed. One more
mf
8vb
star, one more stripe. Join the blue, the white, and red. One more
(8vb)
star, one more stripe, as you pray your child's not

dead...
With the
f sharply accented
With a beat
roof leak-ing, and the walls wet-ter, and the
mf
night as black as
pitch. With the wind shriek-ing, and his
f
mp like an echo

last
let - ter
says he's
fight
-
ing
in
a
f
mp
ditch.
Then the
can
-
dle
flick - ers
and the
riv
-
er
bick - ers,
What else
can
you
do
but
2
stitch
one
more

star,
one
more
stripe,
'til
you
f
8vb
feel
the
ris
-
ing
sun?
One
more
(8vb)
star,
one
more
stripe,
'til
this
(8vb)
fool
-
ish
-
ness
is
done.
One
more
(8vb)

star, one more stripe. Who'll be wait - ing when we've
won? Grab a
ff
nee-dle, grab a thim - ble if it's all that keeps you sane. Think of
f
free-dom as a sym - bol, think of jus - tice as a gain! Think of

life with in - de - pen - dence, think of mus - kets and bri - gades, think of
tak - ing the op - pres - sors, think of ban - ners and pa - rades! When the
gate creaks and the paint cracks and the cat cries and the night crawls, raise a
sub. p
flag! Raise a flag! Raise a
8va
f

flag 'til you're free!! One more
(8va)
ff
star, one more stripe, 'til this blood - shed's fin - 'lly through! One more
fff
8vb
star, one more stripe 'til they come back home to you! One more
(8vb)
star, one more stripe, when there's
f

nothing you can do!
fff
If they take all the things that define what you were and are…
mp
sharply accented
mp
one more…
star…
mp

FROM CHOPIN TO COUNTRY

from *Cowgirls*

Written by MARY MURFITT
Enhanced by FRÉDÉRIC CHOPIN

B♭sus
B♭
E♭
1
I could have been in Hei - del - berg by now. From
I could have been in Liech - ten - stein by now.
I could have been in Dus - sel - dorf by now.
2,3
B♭
F/A
I think I hear a lar -
So, I'll just play par - ti -
A♭
E♭/G
go ar - riv - ing by Wells Far -
tas while red - necks eat fa - ji -
Edim7
F7
go. I'd ride for miles by po -
tas. Top off your Tex - as wie -

To Coda
Gm7
Cm7
F
B♭
B/A
E/G♯
ny
just
to hear a sym - pho - ny
nie with ketch - up
and Puc - ci - ni
rit.
C7/G
F7
B♭7
D.S. al Coda
(take 2nd ending)
(ee.)
From
a tempo
CODA
(ee.)
From
E♭
B♭
E♭
Cho - pin to coun - try, it's
a tempo
C
Fm
real - ly quite per - func - t'ry. We're

B♭
Bdim
Cm
Adim
so glad to be here; we're tick - led and how.
B♭sus
B♭
B♭sus
B♭
I could have been in Hei - del - berg, I could have been in Liech - ten - stein,
B♭sus
B♭
Fast
N.C.
E♭
B♭
I could have been in Dus - sel - dorf
rall.
E♭
B♭
E♭
by now.

GIMME GIMME
from *Thoroughly Modern Millie*

Music by JEANINE TESORI
Lyrics by DICK SCANLAN

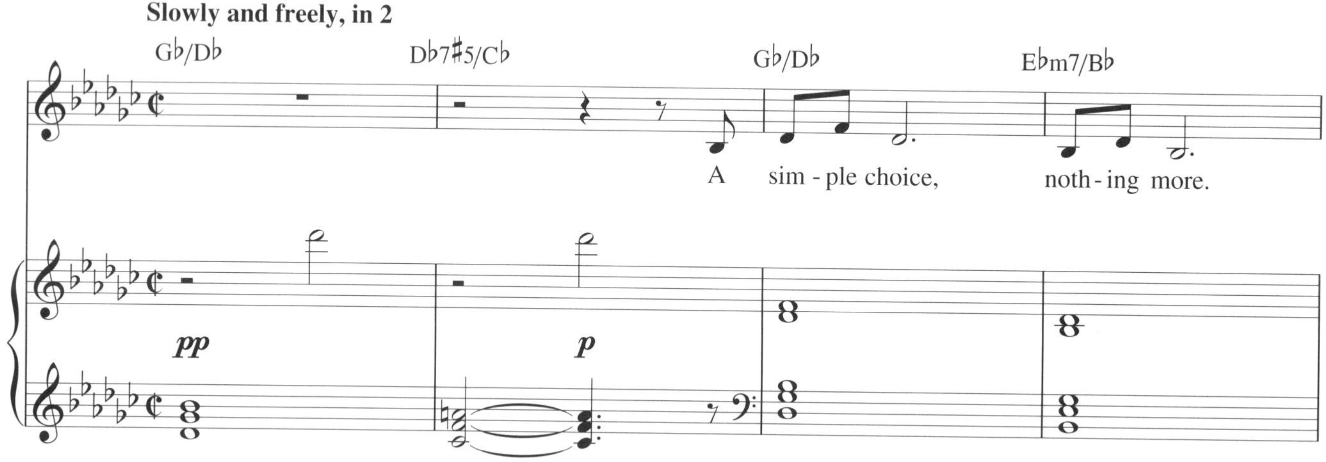

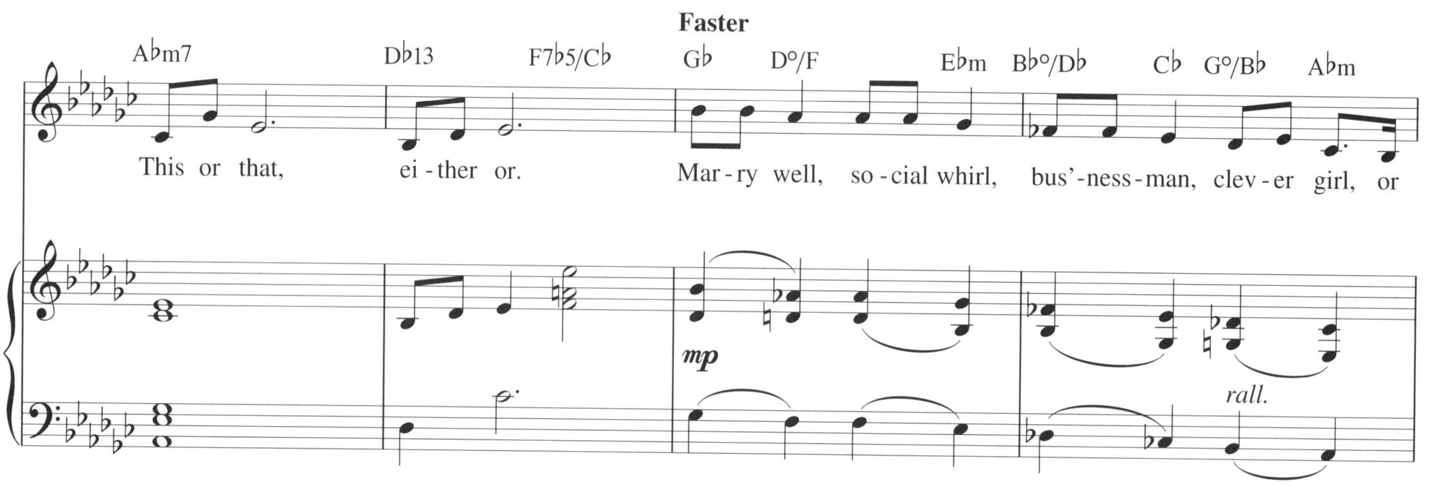

Moderately slow (♫ = ♩♪) (not a wide swing)
N.C.
E6/B
B+add2
E6/B
I say:
Gim-me gim-me…
Gim-me gim-me…
B+add2
E6/B
B+add2
E6/B
Gim-me gim-me
that thing called
love.
B+add2
E6/B
B+add2
E
E/D♯
I want it.
Gim-me gim-me
that thing called
love.
C♯9
C♯9/E♯
F♯7
C7
E/B
I need it.
Highs and lows,
tears and laugh-ter.
Gim-me
hap-py

C♯7
F♯9
B13
C♯m7
E/B
C♯m7
ev - er af - ter.
Gim-me gim-me
that thing called
love.
Moderately, with more confidence
B+
B+/C♯
B+
E
B+add2
E
Gim-me gim-me
that thing called
love.
B+add2
E
B+add2
E
E/D
I crave it.
Gim-me gim-me
that thing called
love.
grad. accel.
C♯7
F♯9
C7
E/B
I'll brave it.
Thick 'n' thin,
rich
or poor time.
Gim-me years and

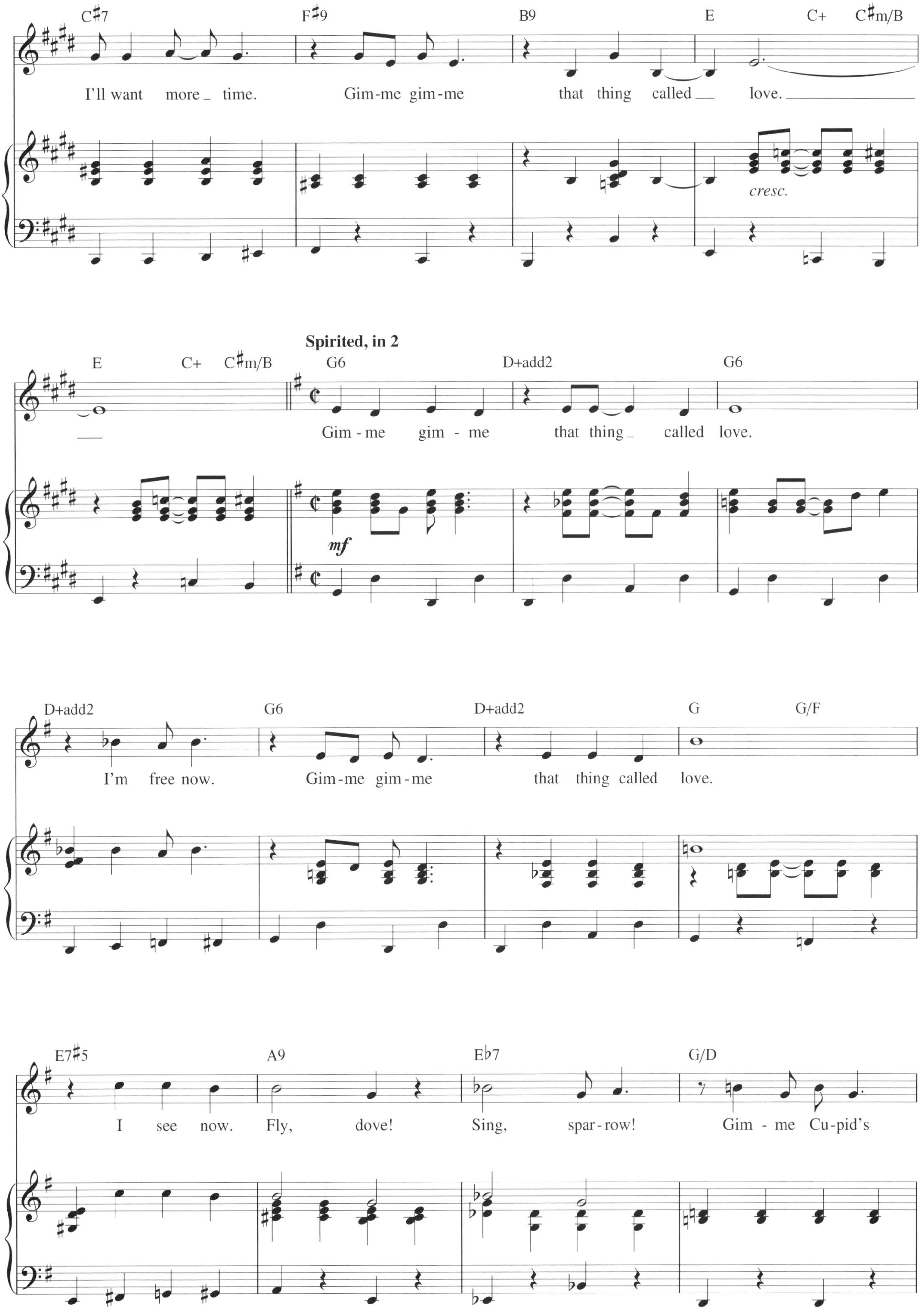

C♯7 F♯9 B9 E C+ C♯m/B

I'll want more _ time. Gim-me gim-me that thing called _ love. ___

cresc.

Spirited, in 2

E C+ C♯m/B G6 D+add2 G6

Gim - me gim - me that thing _ called love.

mf

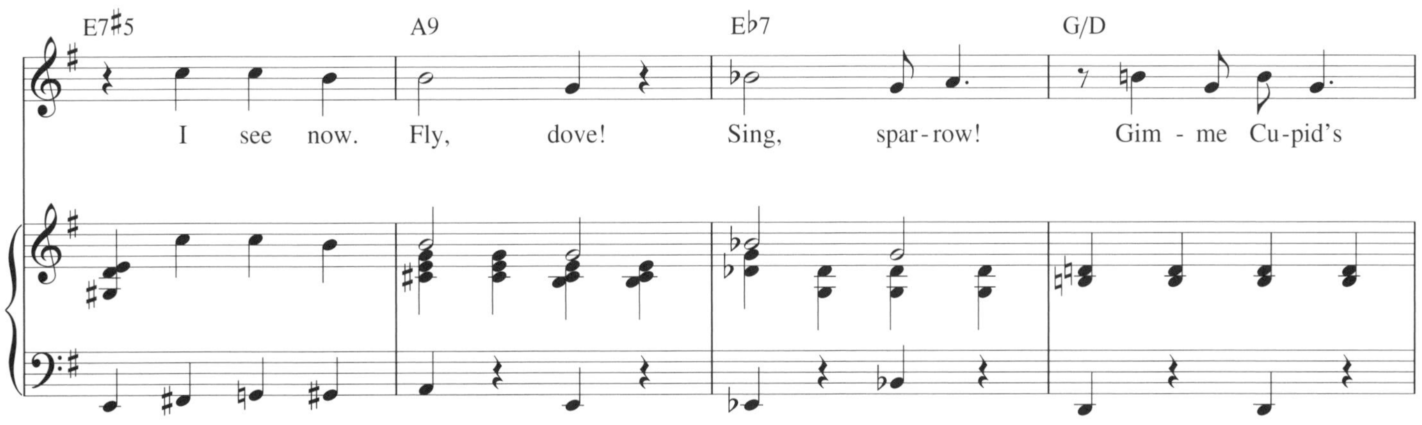

E7
A7
D9
G6
fa - mous ar - row.
Gim-me gim-me
that thing called
love.
Faster
G♯7
G7
G♯7
C♯m
I don't care
if he's a no -
cresc.
f
B♭7
A7
B♭7
E♭m
bod - y.
In my heart
he'll be a some -
B/D♯
D7
bod - y,
some -
bod - y
to love

F6/C
C+add2
F6/C
me.
ff
C9♯5
F6/C
C9♯5
F
F/E♭
I need it.
Gim-me
that thing called
love.
molto rit.
Freely
D7♯5
N.C.
I wan-nit!
Moderately and broadly, in 4 (Bring it home!)
G7
D♭7
F/C
Here I am,
Saint Val-en-tine!
My bags are packed;
Faster
D7
B♭6
D♭7/C♭
F/C
I'm first in line.
Aph-ro-di-te,
don't for-get me.
Ro-me-o and
accel.
mf
8vb

D7
B♭6
B♭m6
F/C
N.C.
Ju - li - et me! Fly, dove! Sing, spar-row! Gim - me fat boy's
cresc.
f
D7
G9
C9
fa - mous ar-row! Gim - me gim - me that thing
F6
F6/E♭
Dm7♭5
D♭7
C9
F6
F6/E♭
called love!
ff
Dm7♭5
D♭7
C9
F6
F6/E♭
Dm7♭5
D♭7
C9
E/C
F

HOW DID WE COME TO THIS?

from *The Wild Party*

Words and Music by
ANDREW LIPPA

F♯m7♭5
G♯m7
C♯13♯9
neigh - bor,
smil - ing through a
hiss.
F♯m9
A(add9)/B
Am(add9)/B
G♯7♭5
C♯m7
How
did
we
come
to
this?
F♯m7
B7sus
B(♭9♭5)
E
E+
We're all
a - mused,
rit.
a tempo
keep it moving
8vb
E
Emaj7♯5
C♯m/E
E+
we're all
in - spired.
So
cun - ning,
so
clev - er,
(8vb)

E
D/E
E9
A(add9)
and so ad - mired.
Eas - y to be
mf
(8vb)
F♯m7♭5
G♯m9
C♯7♯9
an - gry,
eas - y to dis - miss.
(8vb)
F♯m9
B7sus
E
How did we come to this?
mp
mf
(8vb)
D♯m7♭5
G♯m7♭9
G♯m7/C♯
C♯m7
G♯m7/C♯
C♯m7
D♯m7♭5
G♯m7♭9
G♯m7♯9
May - be I've been liv - ing in a day - dream.
May - be I've been talk - ing in my
f
8vb
8vb

C♯maj7
F♯m7
F♯m7/B
Emaj7
Amaj7
sleep.
If I've been a - wake,
par - don my mis - take,
8vb
D♯m7♭5
C7♭5
rit.
B6/9
D7sus/B
E
but time is run - ning low and
talk is grow - ing cheap.
We play our
E+
E
G♯/E
C♯m/E
games.
We place out
bets.
No wit - ness,
(8vb)
D6/E
E9
A(add9)
no weak - ness,
and no re - grets.
Fill - ing up with

F♯m7♭5
G♯m9
C♯+(♯9) C♯7+(♭9) F♯m7(add11)
F♯m9
fren - zy.
Kill-ing with a kiss.
How did we
(8vb)
8vb
Slower
B
B7
B7♯5/A
G♯m7♭5
Bm/C♯
C♯7
F♯9
D9♯11
all come to this?
Time goes by, plans grow stale,
rit.
ff
8vb
8vb
Very slow
G♯m9
C♯7♭9
F♯m9
B7sus
peo - ple die and par - ties fail.
How did we come to
rit.
p
colla voce
E
D9
E6
this?
move along
poco rit.
mf
mp
8vb

GOOD MORNING BALTIMORE

from *Hairspray*

Music by MARC SHAIMAN
Lyrics by MARC SHAIMAN and SCOTT WITTMAN

Medium '60s Rock

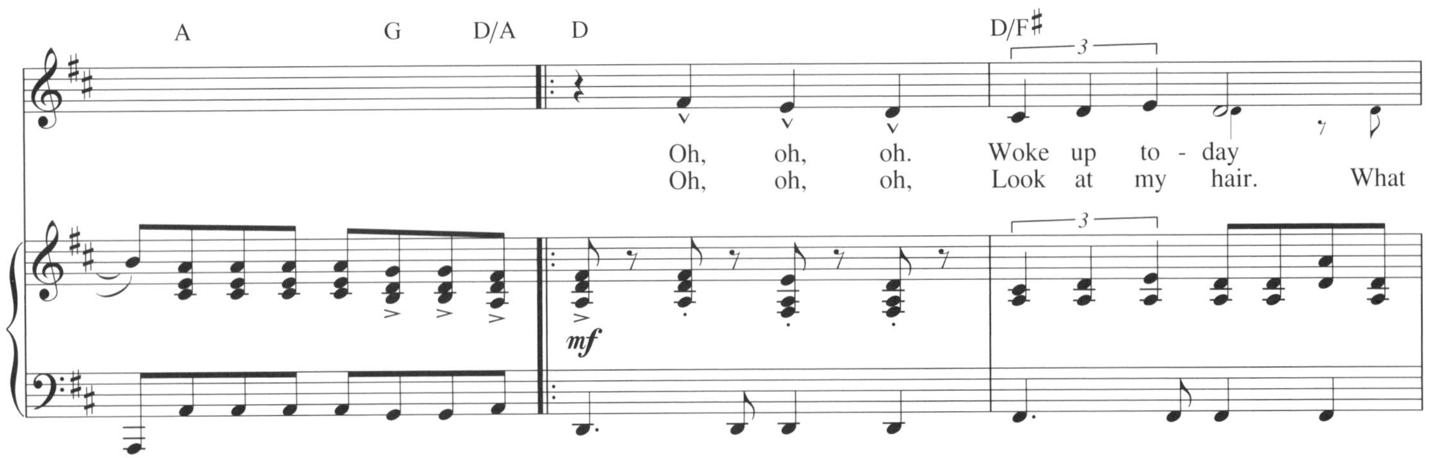

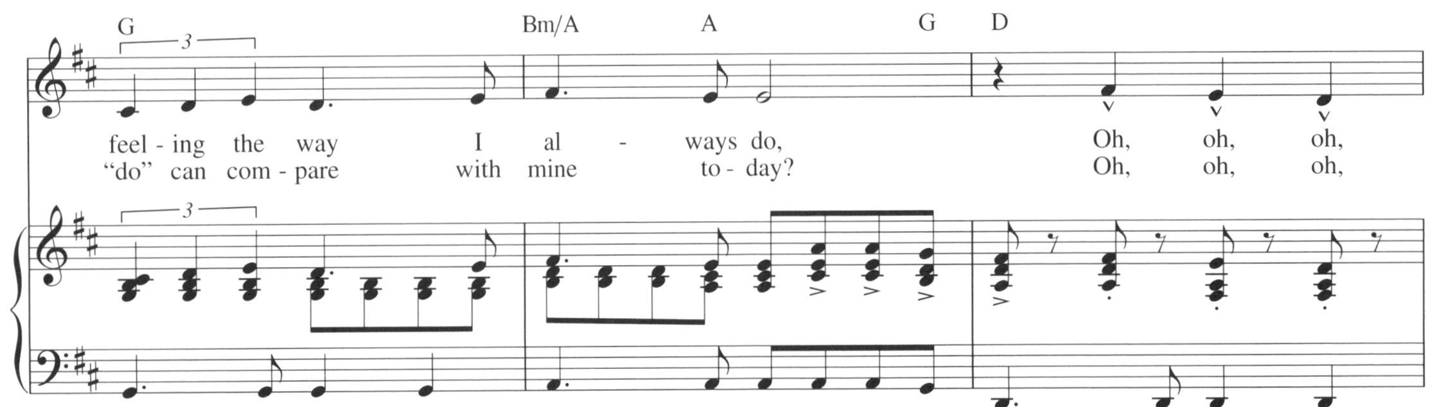

Bm
Gm/B♭
B♭7
D/A
rhy - thm of town starts call - ing me down. It's like a mes - sage from
rats on the streets all dance'round my feet. They seem to say, "Tra - cy, it's
G♯m7♭5
E/G♯
D/A
A
D/A
high a - bove Oh, oh, oh, Pull - ing me out to the
up to you." So, oh, oh, Don't hold me back,'cause to -
G
Em9
A
D/A
A7
Dsus 2/4
D
smiles and the streets that I love. Good morn - ing, Bal - ti - more!
day all my dreams will come true. Good morn - ing, Bal - ti - more!
f
G(add9)
G
Ev - 'ry day's like an o - pen door. Ev - ry night is a
There's the flash - er who lives next door. There's the bum on his
3

Dsus
D
D/A
Asus
fan - ta - sy.
bar - room stool.
Ev - 'ry sound's like a sym - pho - ny.
They wish me luck on my way to school.

A
D/A
A7
Dsus 2/4
D
D7/C
Good morn - ing, Bal - ti - more!
And some day when I

G/B
Gm/B♭
D/A
take to the floor, the world's gon - na wake up and _ see

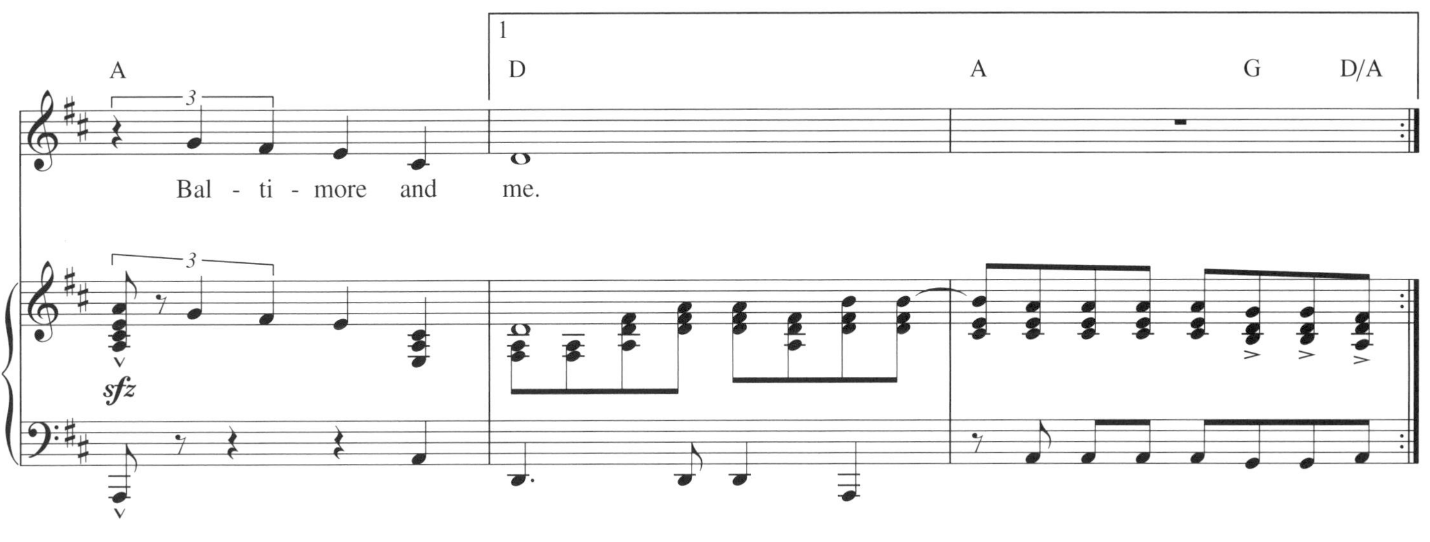
1
A
D
A
G
D/A
Bal - ti - more and me.
sfz

2
D
B♭
me.
I know ev - 'ry step. I
mp

F/A
Gm7
Gm/A
F/A
know ev - 'ry song. I know there's a place where I be - long. I

C
G/B
Am7
G/B
see all those par - ty lights shin - ing a - head. So some - one in - vite me be -
f
Asus
A
D
fore I drop dead!
So, oh, oh,
ff
mf
D/F♯
G
Bm/A
A
G
Give me a chance, 'cause when I start to dance I'm a mo - vie star.
D
D/F♯
G♯m7♭5
E/G♯
Oh, oh, oh, Some-thing in - side of me makes me move when

F♯7♭9/A♯
Bm
Gm/B♭
B♭7
I hear the groove. My ma tells me, "No," but my feet tell me, "Go."
D/A
G♯m7♭5
E/G♯
It's like a drum - mer in - side my heart.
D/A
A
D/A
G
Em7
Oh, oh, oh, Don't make me wait one more mo - ment for my life to
mf
D/A
A7sus
D/A
A7sus
B♭7sus
start.

B♭ E♭/B♭ B♭7 E♭sus 2/4 E♭
I love you, Bal - ti - more! Ev - 'ry day's like an
ff
A♭2 A♭ E♭sus E♭
o - pen door. Ev - 'ry night is a fan - ta - sy.
E♭/B♭ B♭sus B♭ E♭/B♭ B♭7
Ev - 'ry sound's like a sym - pho - ny. And I pro - mise,
E♭sus 2/4 E♭ E♭7/D♭ A♭/C
Bal - ti - more, that some day when I take to the floor, the

A♭m/C♭
E♭/B♭
world's gon-na wake up and see,
Am7♭5
A♭/B♭
B♭
gon-na wake up and see
Bal-ti-more and
sfz
E♭
E♭sus
E♭
B♭9
E♭
E♭sus
E♭
me.
Bal-ti-more and me,
B♭
B♭
A♭(add9)
E♭
Bal-ti-more and me!
rit.

HOW CAN I LOSE YOU?

from *Myths and Hymns*

Music and Lyrics by
ADAM GUETTEL

day after day? I look around now, you're what I see.
Pictures of you leaving me. No one should always lose.
mf
Can't I find some kind of peace? Nobody owns the
blues, but I have a long term lease. I

nev - er know why, I nev - er know when. I'm go - ing a - long, it
hap - pens a - gain. I have a blind spot for - ty miles wide.
I have a ter - ri - ble weak - ness in - side! That's how I lose you.
That's how I lose you.

Violin Solo
I was an - oth - er girl,
joy - ous and hap - py and
free.
She was a per - fect pearl,
mf

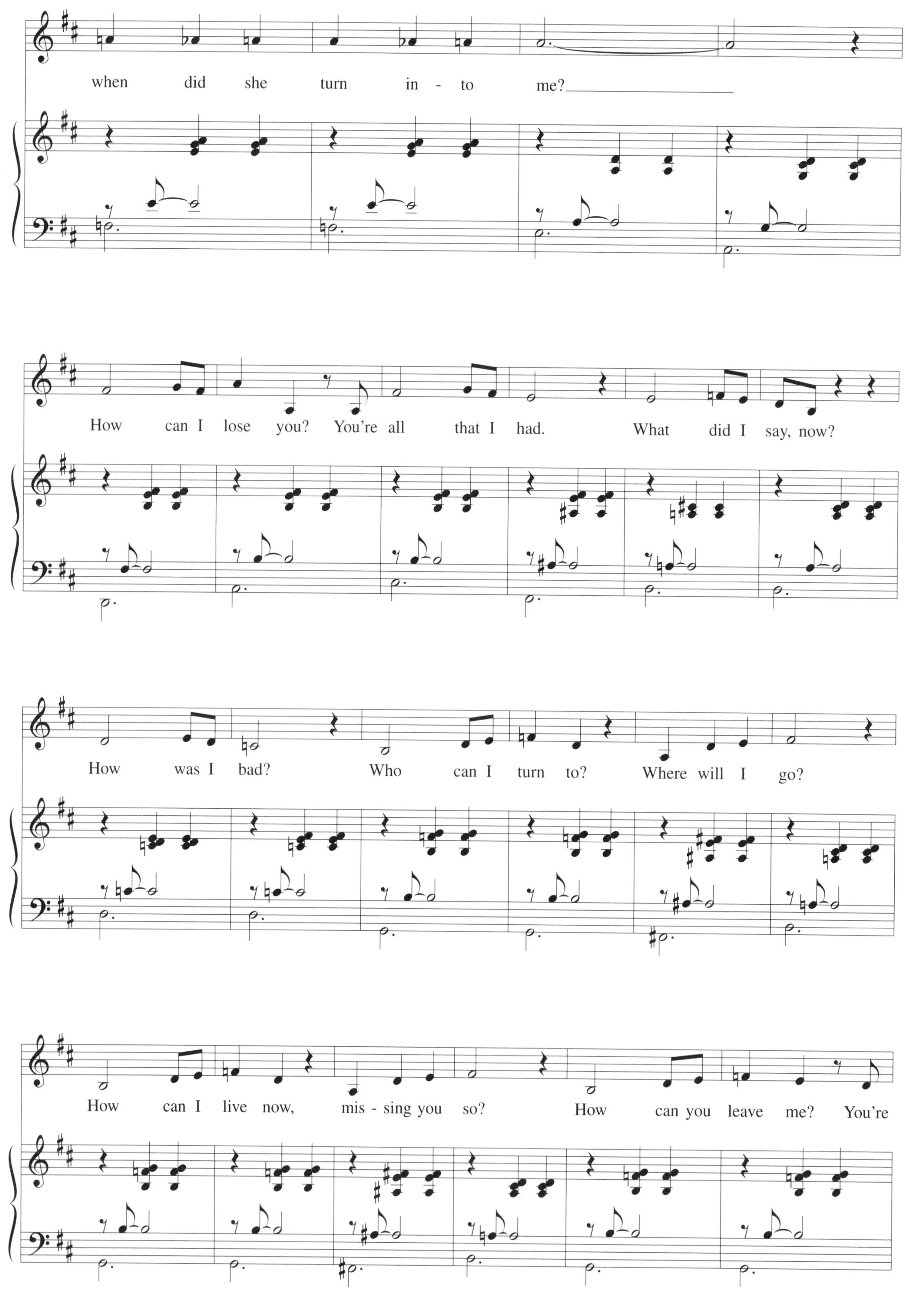

when did she turn in - to me?

How can I lose you? You're all that I had. What did I say, now?

Slower, rubato
all that I know! Oh! That's how I lost you!
That's how I al - ways lost you. That's how I'll al - ways lose you...
In tempo
Violin Solo
Oh.

I CAN DO BETTER THAN THAT

from *The Last Five Years*

Music and Lyrics by
JASON ROBERT BROWN

A2
F♯m11
Ca-rol-ann get-tin' big-ger ev-'ry min-ute, think-in', "What am I do-in' here?"
mp
DMaj9
A2
While Mitch-ell's out ev-'ry night be-in' a hea-vy me-tal drum-mer. They got a
F♯m11
A2/E
D6/9
lit-tle cute house on a lit-tle cute street With a cru-ci-fix on the door,
mf
A2/C♯
D6/9
A2/D♯
B m11/E
Mitch-ell got a job at a re-cord store in the mall. Just the

F♯m11 A2/E D6/9 (3)

ty-pi-cal facts of a ty-pi-cal life in a town on the East-ern shore. I

A2/C♯ A2/D A2/C♯ F♯m/D♯

thought a-bout what I wan-ted, It was-n't like that at all... Made

mp

A2/E F♯m11 Bm11 D6/9 D/E

Ca-rol-ann a cute ba-by sweat-er, think-in' "I can do bet-ter than

A2 F♯m11

that."

mf

DMaj9
Bm11
A2
F♯m11
In a year or so, I moved to the ci-ty, think-in', "What have I got to lose?"
mp
DMaj9
Bm11
Bm11/E
Got a room, got a cat, and got twen-ty pounds thin-ner.
A2
F♯m11
3
Met a guy in a class I was tak-ing who, you might say, looked like Tom Cruise.

DMaj9
A2
He would-n't leave me a - lone 'less I went with him to din-ner.
And I
mf
F♯m11
A2/E
D6/9
guess he was cute, and I guess he was sweet, and I guess he was good in bed:
I
A2/C♯
D6/9
A2/D♯
Bm11/E
gave up my life for the bet-ter part of a year.
So I'm
F♯m11
A2/E
D6/9
start-ing to think that this may - be might work, and the se-cond it en-tered my head,
He

A2/C♯
A2/D
A2/C♯
need - ed to take some time off,
Fo - cus on his "ca -
mp
F♯m/D♯
A2/E
F♯m11
Bm11
D6/9
reer." He blew me off with a heart - felt let - ter, I thought,
mf
D/E
A2
"I can do bet - ter than that."
You don't
f
D6/9
Bm11
have to get a hair - cut, You don't have to change your shoes, You don't
mp legato

D6/9
D6/9/E
Asus
A
have to like Du-ran Du-ran, just love me. You don't
D6/9
Bm11
have to put the seat down, You don't have to watch the news, You don't
D6/9
B7/D♯
A6/E
C♯7/E♯
have to learn to tan - go, You don't have to eat pro-sciut - to, You don't
crisper cresc. poco a poco
F♯m
E/F♯
F♯m
F♯m11
B7sus
B7
have to change a thing, Just stay with me!
f

B7sus
B7 A/B
D6/9
I want you and you and noth-ing but you, Mi-
mf
B m11
G6/9
C7(#11)
-les and pi-les of you Fi-nal-ly I'll have some-thing worth-while to think of each
8va
loco
D2
G2
morn-ing: You and you and noth-ing but you! No
E7sus
E9
G2
C7(#11) C9
sub-sti-tu-tion will do, No-thing but fresh, un-di-lu-ted and pure, Top of the

G/A
D/G
D6/F♯
Bm9/E
line,
And to - tal - ly
D/E
E/D
A/C♯
Bm11
Bm7/E
mine!
ff
8vb
A2
F♯m11
I don't need an - y life - time com - mit - ments, I don't need to get hitched to - night,
f
loco
DMaj9
Bm11
I don't want you to throw up all your walls and de - fens - es.

A2
F♯m11
I don't mean to put on an - y pres - sure, but I know when a thing is right,
mp
DMaj9
A2
And I spend ev - 'ry day re - con - fig - u - ring my sens - es.
When we
F♯m11
F♯m11/E
F♯m11/D
get to my house, take a look at that town, Take a look at how far I've gone.
I will
mf
A2/C♯
A2/D
A2/D♯
Esus
nev - er go back, nev - er look back an - y - more.
And it feels

F♯m11
F♯m11/E
F♯m11/D
3
__ like my life led right__ to your side__ and will keep me there__ from now__ on.
A2/C♯
A2/D
A2/C♯
A2/D
Think a-bout what you__ wan - ted,
Think a - bout what could__ be,______
mp
A2/C♯
A2/D
A2/C♯
F♯m/D♯
Think a - bout how__ I________ love__ you__ and say__ you'll move in with__ me.
A2/E
F♯m11
A2/E
F♯m11
Think of what's great a - bout me and you,__
Think__ of the bull - shit we've both been through, Think__
mf

A2/E
F♯m11
G6/9
of what's past, be-cause we can do Bet - ter!
f
Bm7/E
We can do bet - ter!
D/E
A2/D
A/C♯
We can do bet - ter than that!
ff
Bm9
A/C♯
D6/9
D/E
A
We can do bet - ter than that!
8va
(l.v.)
sfz

I KNOW THE TRUTH

from Elton John and Tim Rice's *Aida*

Music by ELTON JOHN
Lyrics by TIM RICE

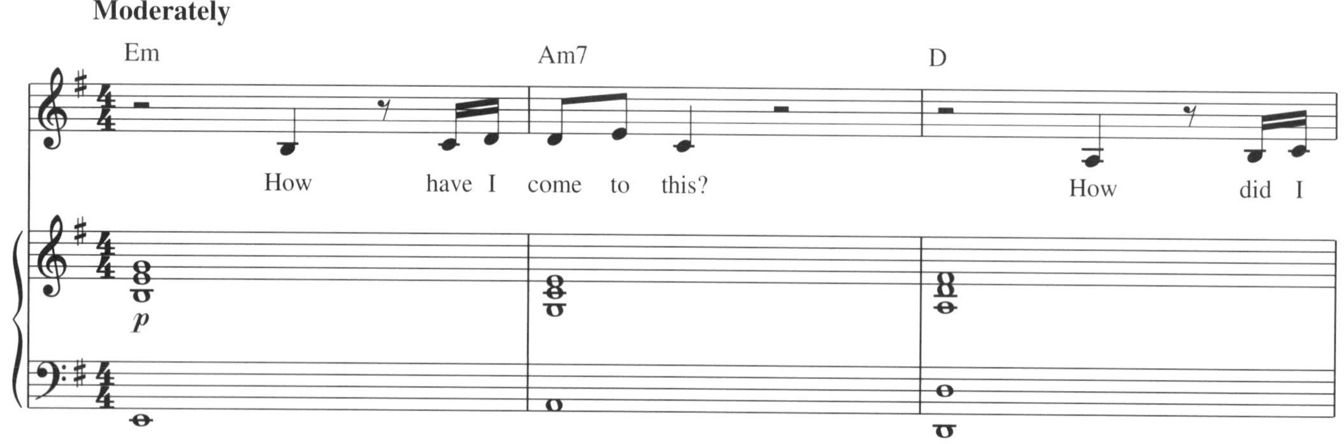

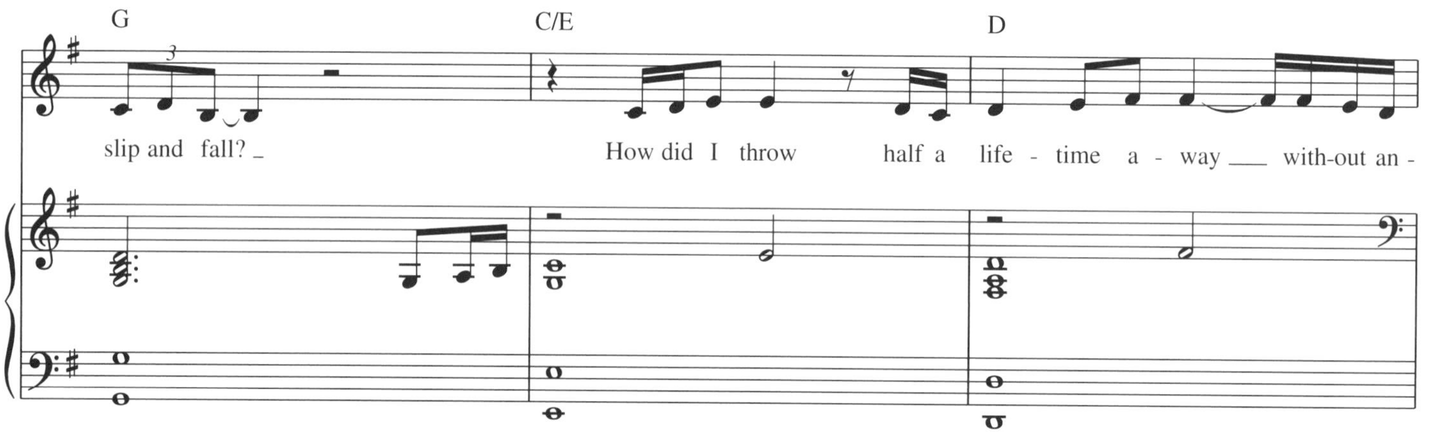

Am7
D
G
been my time
It's o - ver it nev - er be - gan
C/E
D
I closed my eyes to so much for so long and I no
G
C/G
G
F/A
G/B
long - er can
I try to blame it on
C
D
Bm
for - tune
Some kind of shift in a star

Em
Am7
D
But I know the truth and it haunts me
It's flown just a lit - tle too
G
F/A
G/B
C
far
I know the truth and it mocks me
D
Bsus
B
I know the truth and it shocks me
Em
Am7
Cmaj7/D
D
It's flown just a lit - tle too

C/G
G
D/F♯
Em
far
Why do I
p
Am7
D7sus
D
G
want him still?
Why when there's noth-ing there?
C/E
D
G
C/G
3
How to go on with the rest of my life To pre-tend I don't care?
G
Em
Am7
This ___ should have been my time __ It's

D
G
C/E
o - ver it nev - er be - gan
3
3
I closed my eyes to so
D
G
F/A
G/B
much for so long and I no long - er can
I try to blame it on
C
D
Bm
for - tune
Some kind of twist in my fate
Em
Am7
D
But I know the truth and it haunts me
I learned it a lit - tle too

G
F/G
G
C
late
I know the truth _ and it mocks me ___
f
D/C
Bsus
B
Em
I know the truth _ and it shocks me ________ I
rall.
Rubato
Am7
Dsus
D
Csus2
Gmaj7/B
learned it ______________ a lit - tle too late ____
C(add2)
D
G(add2)
Too late ________________________________

I'M LEAVING YOU
from *The Life*

Music by CY COLEMAN
Lyrics by IRA GASMAN

What-ev - er hap-pened to that dream we used to share? What-ev - er
hap-pened to the love that once was there? What-ev - er hap-pened to
me and you?
poco rall.
a tempo
poco rall.
a tempo
I could take los - ing pride and

los - ing face.
I could take an - y - thing but sec - ond place.
You were the on - ly joy I ev - er knew, but you can save your sweet talk, ba - by,'cause your
ba - by's through be - liev - ing you. I'm
mf
rall.
leav-ing you.
ten.
rall.

I'M NOT
from *Little by Little*

Music by BRAD ROSS
Lyric by ELLEN GREENFIELD

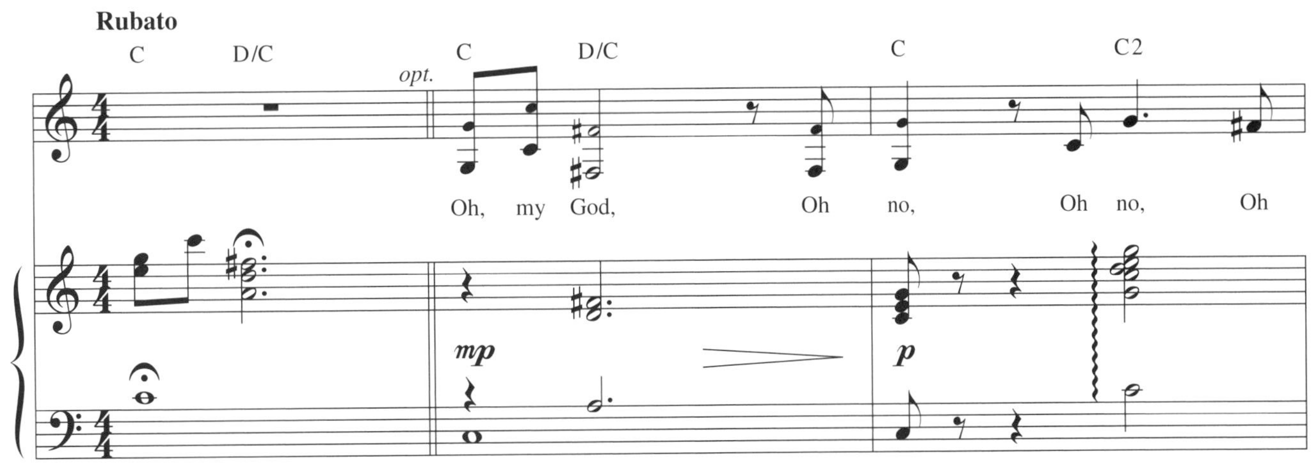

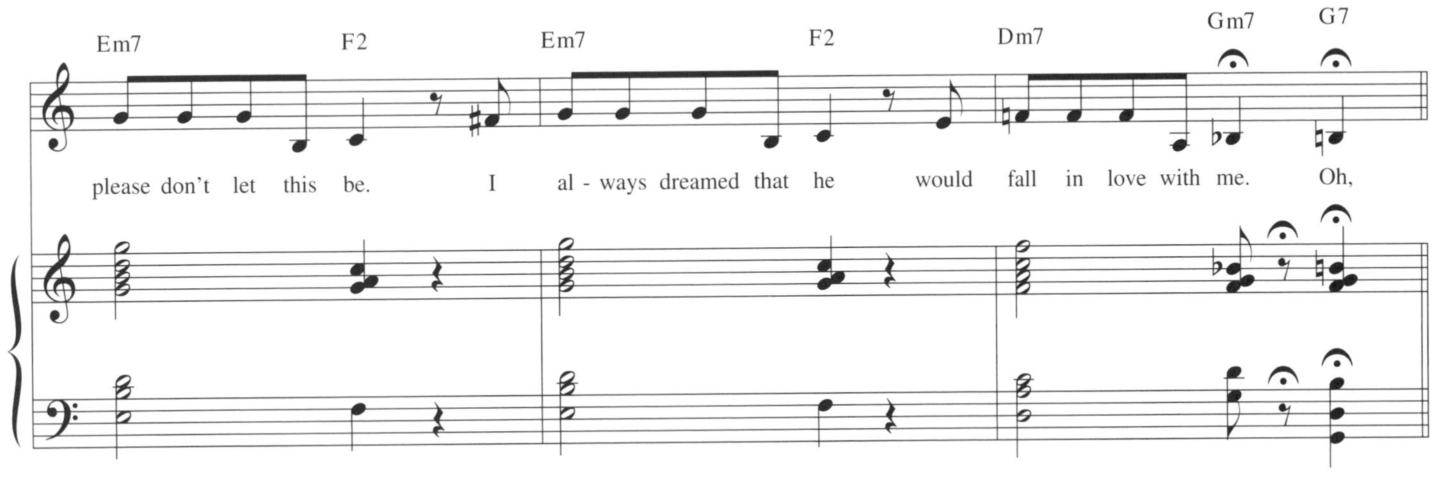

C D/C C D/C C D/C C Csus C
great. And she is, well, to him the per - fect
mp
Gm7/C C Gm7/C C Gm7/C C7 Fsus F
date. I'm not, not as spi - cy, not as
Em11 A7 Dm7 C/D
hot. I'm not. I'm nice which sig - nals
Dm7 C/E F6 D7/F♯ Dm11/G G7
bland, so in de - mand I'm not.

Csus C C D/C C D/C C D/C C
He is, he's ex - cep - tion - al - ly cute. And
Csus C Gm7/C C Gm7/C C
she is, well, his first for - bid - den fruit.
Gm7/C C7 Fsus F Em11
I'm not, not as ripe, I'm not his type, I'm
A7 Dm7 C/D Dm7 C/D
not. No, I'm too nice, too smart, the girl to

Dm7
C/E
F
F/G
Csus
C
Csus
C
C
win his heart I'm not.
I'm
B♭/C
Am7/C
doomed to be their pal. I see my fate now.
My
p
B♭/C
F
G/F
F
G/F
F
G/F F
fool - ish dreams of him I'll put a - way.
Suc -
f
GMaj7/A
A7sus
DMaj7
cess will be my goal, and I can't wait, now,

D7
C2/E
D7/F♯
G7sus4
to hear how they'll say,
C
D/C
C
"Oh my God, We knew her when." As
8va
Em7
F2
Dm11/G
ev - 'ry plan I plan comes true I'll al - ways be so grate - ful to the lit - tle peo - ple I once knew.
p
Dm7/G
Csus
C
C
D/C
C
D/C
'Cause he is, well, the boy that I'll re - call,
f
f

C D/C C
Csus
C
Gm9/C
And she is, well, the girl who has it all.
Fsus
F
I'm not, well not yet, but wait and
G/A
Dm7
see.
I'm not as formed as
p
Em7
G/A
some But I'm not what I'll be - come and be -

Dm7
Dm7/G
lieve me, They'll soon see ex -
f
mp
f
Dm7 C/E F G A♭2 A♭ A♭6 A♭
act - ly what I've got, in -
F C/E Dm7 Dm/G
stead of what I'm
C D/C C D/C C D/C C D/C D/C C
not.
f
ff
sfz

I'M NOT THAT GIRL
from the Broadway Musical *Wicked*

Music and Lyrics by
STEPHEN SCHWARTZ

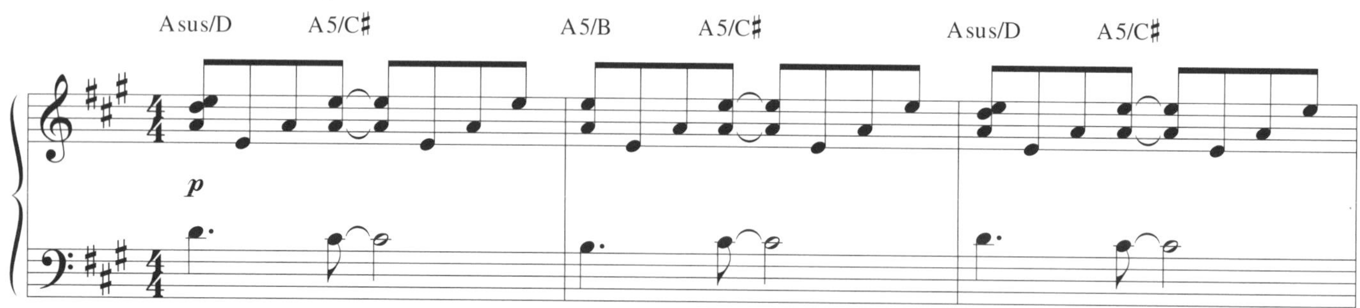

D(add9) D E/G♯ C♯m7 A/C♯ Bm A/D
whirl, He could be that boy, but I'm not that
Esus E Asus/D A5/C♯ A5/B A5/C♯
girl. Don't dream too far,
mp
Asus/D A5/C♯ E/B A D/F♯ F♯m E/G♯
Don't lose sight of who you are. Don't re-mem - ber that rush of
D6/9 D E/G♯ C♯m7 A/C♯ Bm7 A/D
joy. He could be that boy, I'm not that girl.

A
F
B♭/D
E♭
Ev - 'ry so of - ten we long to steal to the
mf
A♭maj7/C
D♭(add9)
Em
A/C♯
land of What-Might - Have - Been,
But that does - n't soft - en the
F♯7/A♯
Bm
C
Bsus
Asus/B♭
E7/B♭
ache we feel when re - al - i - ty sets back in.
poco rit.
Tempo I
Asus/D
A5/D
A5/B
A5/C♯
Asus/D
A5/C♯
Blithe smile,
lithe limb,
She who's win - some,

E/B
A
D/F♯
F♯m
E/G♯
D(add9)
E(add2)/G♯
she wins him.
Gold hair
with a gen-tle
curl
That's the girl he
C♯m7
A/C♯
Bm7
A/D
Esus
chose,
and heav - en
knows,
E
Asus/D
A5/C♯
A5/B
A5/C♯
I'm not
that
girl.
p
Asus/D
A5/C♯
Asus/B
Asus/D
A5/C♯
Don't
wish,
pp

A5/B
A5/C♯
Asus/D
A5/C♯
E/B
A
don't start.
Wish - ing on - ly wounds the heart.
cresc.
A Tempo
D/F♯
F♯m
E/G♯
D(add9)
D
E/G♯
I was - n't born for the rose and pearl,
There's a girl I
mf
rit.
warmly
C♯m7
A/C♯
Bm7
A/D
Esus
know—
He loves her so,
poco rit.
E
Asus/D
A5/C♯
E/B
I'm not that girl...
opt.
a tempo
p
rit.

JUST ONE STEP

from *Songs for a New World*

Music and Lyrics by
JASON ROBERT BROWN

Moderately, but with an edge

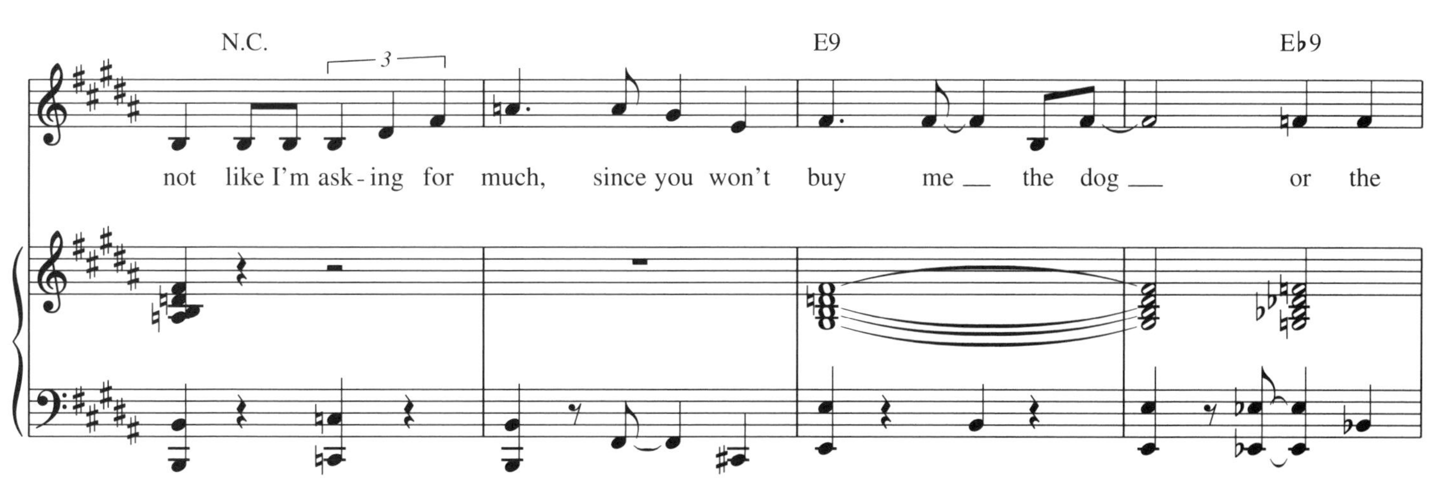

D9
Db9
C9
beach house _ in Quogue (as if you did - n't have the mon - ey...).
B9
What else is new? ___
B7 N.C.
3
I'm not gon-na fight for a coat, so nev - er mind, Mur-ray.
B7
3
E9
If that's what's im-por-tant to you, at least I know where _ I

Eb9
D9
Db9
C9
stand, so Mur-ray, strike up the band! 'Cause the time has come for ac-tion.
F+
Here's what I'll do:
D6/E
E(add2)
D6/E
E5
Clear - ly I'm not want - ed an - y - more,
D6/E
E(add2)
Bm7/E
E7
D6/E
E(add2)
now I'm not so young and beau - ti - ful. That's o - kay.

D6/E
E5
F♯
G/F♯
I've faced de - feat be - fore. I'm not gon-na kvetch and I'm
A♭/F♯
A/F♯
B♭/F♯
B/F♯
C/F♯
C♯/F♯
E7
not gon-na cry. It's not gon-na get me what I want-ed so I'm sim-ply gon-na take one step,
mf
E♭9/E
D9/E
E7
one ti - ny step, and Mur - ray, just one step I'll be
B
C♯m7
Bdim/D
B/D♯
E7
free!
One small step, just so you should - n't
f
mf

Gdim/E
G7/E
F♯
Em/F♯
F/F♯
F♯
Em/F♯
F/F♯
wor - ry, I'll be free and_you'll be rid of me. Is - n't that
p
mf
p
mf
F♯
F♯7♯9
F♯7
B5 N.C.
3
eas - y, Mur - ray? Watch me... You think this is may-be a
joke? Well it's no joke, Mur-ray!
ad lib.
B7
3
Spoken: "Murray?"
Sung: It looks like they're form-ing a crowd, like eight - y -
repeat ad lib.
mp
mf

E9
Eb9
D9
Db9
five, at the most. Still front page of the Post. Mur, I
C9
F+
think it's Mau-ry Po - vich! And Con - nie, too!
D6/E
E(add2)
D6/E
Spoken: "Hi, Connie!"
Sung: Now you'll fi - n'lly make
mf
E5
D6/E
E(add2)
Bm/E
E7
D6/E
your moth - er proud, since she nev - er liked me an -

E(add2) D6/E E5
- y - way. "Look! She's throw - ing dia - monds to the crowd!" You
F♯ G/F♯ A♭/F♯ A/F♯ B♭/F♯ B/F♯
just say the word and I'll come back in - side, but un - til then I'll be hap - py just to
C/F♯ G♯/F♯ E9
know that I can al-ways go and take one step, one ti - ny step. Yes,
mf
E♭9 D9 E7 B C♯m7 Bdim/D B/D♯
Mur - ray, just one step. A - di - os!
f

E7
E9
Gdim/E
G7/E
One small step. Hon - ey, you bet - ter hur - ry!
mf
F♯
Em/F♯
F/F♯
F♯
Em/F♯
F/F♯
Oh, yes sir! Bet - ter give up that fur! Take _ it from
p
p
F♯
F♯7♯9
F♯7
me, ol' Mur - ray, here I...
f
B5 N.C.
Spoken: "Whoops! I almost fell, Murray! The mother of your children splattered across Park Avenue in a bloody heap, Murray. And it's all your... fault!"
Sung: Yes, it's
(1st time only)
mp
repeat ad lib.
ff

E9
Eb9/E
E9
Eb9/E
E9
you who made the mon - ey, cause it's you who owns the store._ So if you don't want to spend_
mf
Eb9/E
E9
A/E E7 A/E
E9
Eb9/E
___ it, that's your right. But it's you who bought the pent - house on the
E9
C#7
3
F#7
fif - ty - sev-enth floor,_ so good - night, cheap - skate, good - night. ___
B N.C.
3
3
___ You think I don't know a - bout her? Well, I do, Mur-ray. You
ff
f

E9
Eb9
think I don't know a-bout that, or the things that _ you say to your
mf
mp
D9
Db9
C9
friends ev - 'ry - day? I'm em - bar-rass-ing. _ I'm fat. I'm de -
mand-ing, I'm con - troll - ing... or what-ev - er.
F+
Per - haps it's true...

D6/E
E(add2)
D6/E
E5
Here's the place where I get what I've earned.
mf
D6/E
E(add2)
Bm7/E
E7
D6/E
Why keep cry - ing? Why be mis - 'ra - ble?
E(add2)
D6/E
E5
Look - it, Mu - ray: Some - bod - y's con - cerned!
F♯
G/F♯
A♭/F♯
A/F♯
F♯
G/F♯
A♭/F♯
A/F♯
Trust in the wind and I'll land on the crowd.
No more com-plain-ing I'm trash - y or loud.
subito mp

F♯ G/F♯ A♭/F♯ A/F♯ D/F♯ B/F♯ F♯7♭5 F♯maj7
What a sen-sa-tion-al fuck-ing ex-per-i-ence! Fi-nal-ly Mur-ray! I'm get-ting at-ten-tion! And
E9 A/E E7
just one step! Look at where one step leads you: One small step
8va
loco
ff
B C♯m7 Bdim/D B/D♯ B C♯m7 Bdim/D B/D♯
takes you high!
8va
ff
E9 A7/E G7/E F♯
Just one step down from the man who needs you! Fuck the
loco
mp

Em/F♯ F/F♯ F♯ Em/F♯ F/F♯ F♯
fur: Just_ send it back to her! So,_ fare thee well, and Mur - ray,
F♯7♯9 F♯7 B N.C.
watch me fly!
Vamp
(Vamp till out of breath) Spoken:
"Murray! I'm serious. Murray! Murray?" (GASP!)
Vamp
subito p

JUST LIKE YOU
from *John & Jen*

Music by ANDREW LIPPA
Lyrics by THOMAS GREENWALD

2
way he sleeps with his arm tucked un-der his neck, it's so
true he sleeps just like you.
rit.
Animato - in 2
Animato - in 2
mp
rit.
4
You're com - plete - ly in the shade now. It's a -
ma - zing the way this tree grew.
2
legato

Expansive
Things get so big,
time flies a - way.
Hey, hap - py thir - ty - two.
f
dim.
rit.
I brought you a pre - sent.
rit.
a tempo
He looks just like you.
To -
mp
cresc.

Pesante
mor-row he's go-ing to camp, and I can't
mf
deal with it.
I've
bare-ly ev-er let him out of my sight.
I know that it's just the start

now that he's grow-ing up.
leav-ing home taking
flight
(♩=♪)
You should see this kid your name-sake. I
won-der back when I did that if I knew that ev'-ry

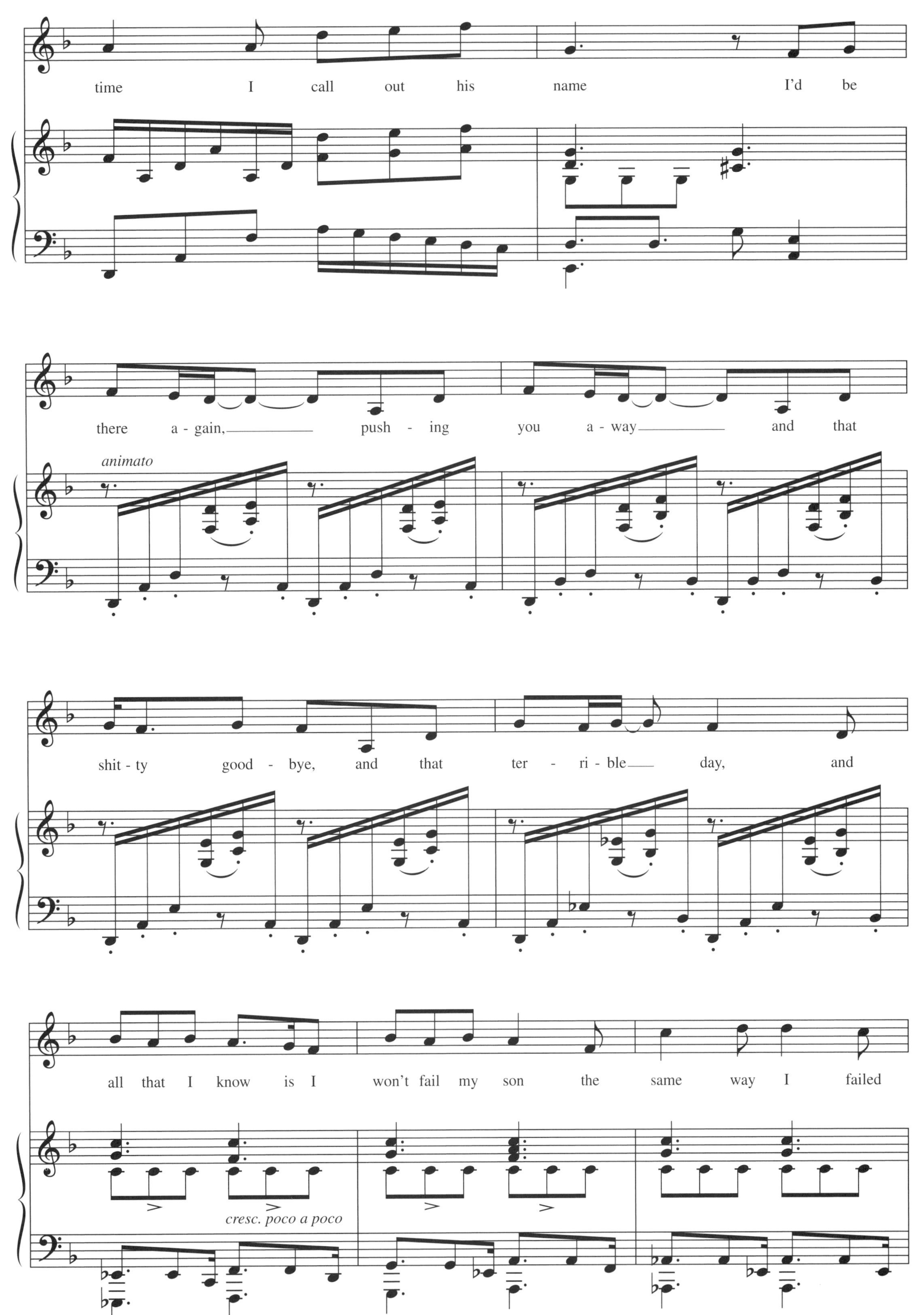
time I call out his name I'd be
there a - gain, push - ing you a - way and that
animato
shit - ty good - bye, and that ter - ri - ble day, and
all that I know is I won't fail my son the same way I failed
cresc. poco a poco

N.B.
you.
Should see this
kid
I wish you could see this kid.
But that's
just like you, you al - ways talked back.
gliss.
You al-ways fought back.
You're not com - ing

back_____ but I won't let my

cresc.

mp *gently*

rit.

ba - by leave me too. No, I won't let him___

rit.

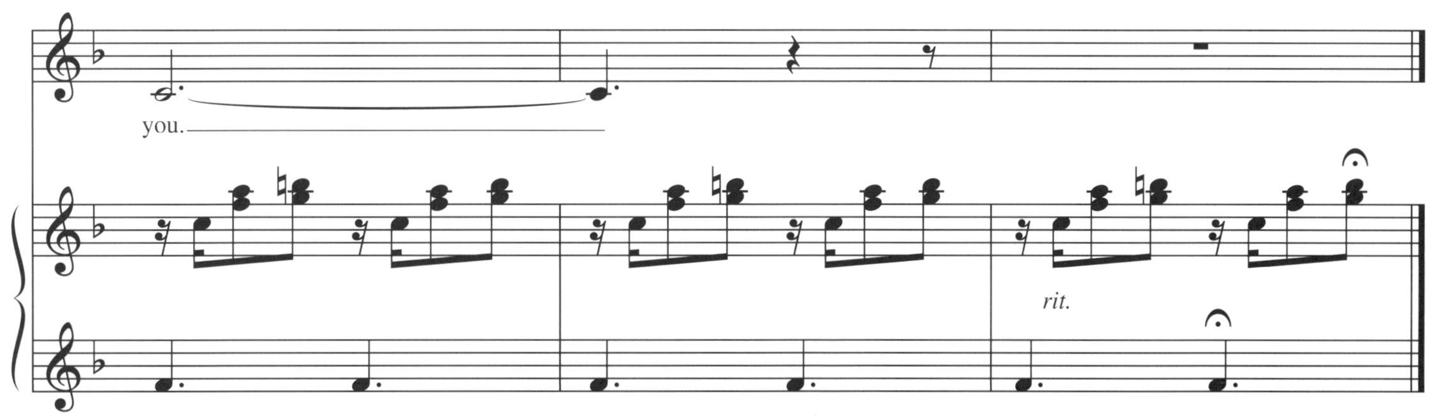

THE LIFE OF THE PARTY

from *The Wild Party*

Words and Music by
ANDREW LIPPA

*The accents are very light in this section.

A Tempo
E(♯9)
A7
D9
Don't you wan - na land the role of a life - time? Well, you bet - ter
8vb
A
E/G♯
F♯7♯9
B7
A7/C♯
get down on one knee. 'Cause you could play the
sim.
D
D♯dim7
C/E
N.C.
life of the par - ty if you can pray with me.
even 8th's

A6 D7 Bbmaj7 A E7#5
Who needs lov-ers? Not I. Who needs heav-en a-bove?
swing
D#m7b5 G7/D7 G#/C#7 A F7 E7
Don't have time for things un-said, for
Eb13 D7 C#7 C7 Bbmaj7 A6 D7
bak-ing bread, for love. All I need is room to fight,
A6 C#7 C#7/E# F#m7 G9
hand in fist-ed glove. Point me to the sky.

C13
N.C.
A7
It's my turn to fly. Don't you wan - na be the life of the par -
D9
A7
D9
- ty? Don't you wan - na be the top of the heap? This is where the
sim.
8vb
8vb
A
E/G♯
A/G
F♯7
B9
jam - bo - ree nev - er ends, why not be count-ing friends in - stead of count-ing sheep?
E(♯9)
A7
D9
If you wan - na join the heav - en - ly choir, hur - ry up and
8vb
8vb

A
E/G#
F#7#9
Bm7
A/C#
D
D#dim7
get your - self in line. But don't you pass the life of the par - ty un -
C/E
N.C.
A7#9
D13
G7#9
C13
til you pass the wine! Let the drinks pour. Let the crowds roar.
A7♭5/B
A7♭9/B♭
Let the heav - ens wild - ly cheer.
A7#9/E
G#7#9/E
'Til the sun - rise brings the good - byes I'll be

B9 N.C.
improvise vocal fills
here ne - ver fear. _
f
p
cresc.
Pull back
Slower
F+/B A7/F
Bb7 Eb7
Who's it gon - na be? The life of the par -
ff
N.C. Bb7 Eb13 N.C.
accel.
- ty. ___ Who's it gon - na be? The king of the hill. Don't you wan - na
accel.
Bb7 A13 Ab7b5 Gm7 C13/Bb E7+ F7+
be there run - ning the show ___ un - til it's time to go ___ or til it's time to kill?

a tempo
F7
Bb7
Eb9
Don't you wan - na be some - bo - dy to en - vy? Don't you wan - na
improvise solo
p
a tempo
Bb7 A7+ Ab7 G7#9 Cm7 Eb/D
be foot - loose and free? Well, you could be the
3
Ebmaj7 Em7b5 Gm7 Db/F F#m/F F+
life of the par - ty if you were more like
sfz
f
gliss.
N.C.
Bb7
me!

MAYBE I LIKE IT THIS WAY

from *The Wild Party*

Words and Music by
ANDREW LIPPA

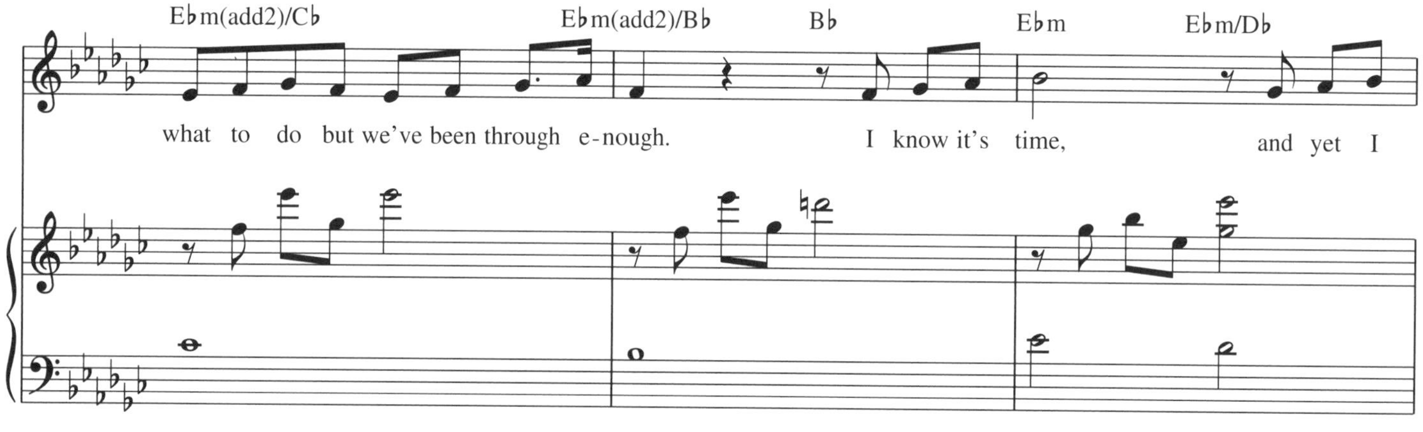

Ebm(add2)
Gb/Db
Abm/Cb
pain, I hear his cry, he pulls me to the edge but I don't ask him
Ab/Bb
Bb7
Ebm
Ebm/Db
Ab/C
Abm/Cb
why. I un - der - stand, and I o - bey,
Con moto
Fb/Bb
Bbsus
Bb
Ebm(add2)
Cb
Db
May - be I like it this way. I like the way he laughs, the way he combs his
Ebm(add2)
Cbm6
Db
hair. I like the way he moves, the way he's al - ways

B♭/D
B♭
E♭/G
A♭
D♭/A♭
there. The way he calls my name, the way he
f
G♭
C♭/E♭
Fm7♭5
B♭7sus
B♭7
takes con - trol. I like the way this man has stirred my soul.
F♯m(add2)
C♯7/E♯
A/E
Spoken: When I first met Burrs, he was grand. You understand? I was
p
D♯m7♭5
Bm9
C♯7/E♯
Amaj7
scared and awful lonely. Hungry and hopeful. How could I know?
mf

Building
F
F(♭5)
Asus/E
A/E
F(♭5)
F
May - be to - mor - row it comes crash - ing down.
May - be next week I'll find an -
Asus/E
A/E
F
G/F
A/E
oth - er clown.
May - be I'll try to go a diff' - rent way,
D♯m7♭5
A♭/B♭
G♭/B♭
Big pull back
A♭/B♭ Fm6/B♭ A♭/B♭ Fm/B♭
but look who's sit - ting here to - day!
If I could
crescendo
E♭m(add2)
G♭6/9/D♭
A♭m/C♭
change, if I could grow,
I'd ask for noth - ing more and through the door I'd
f

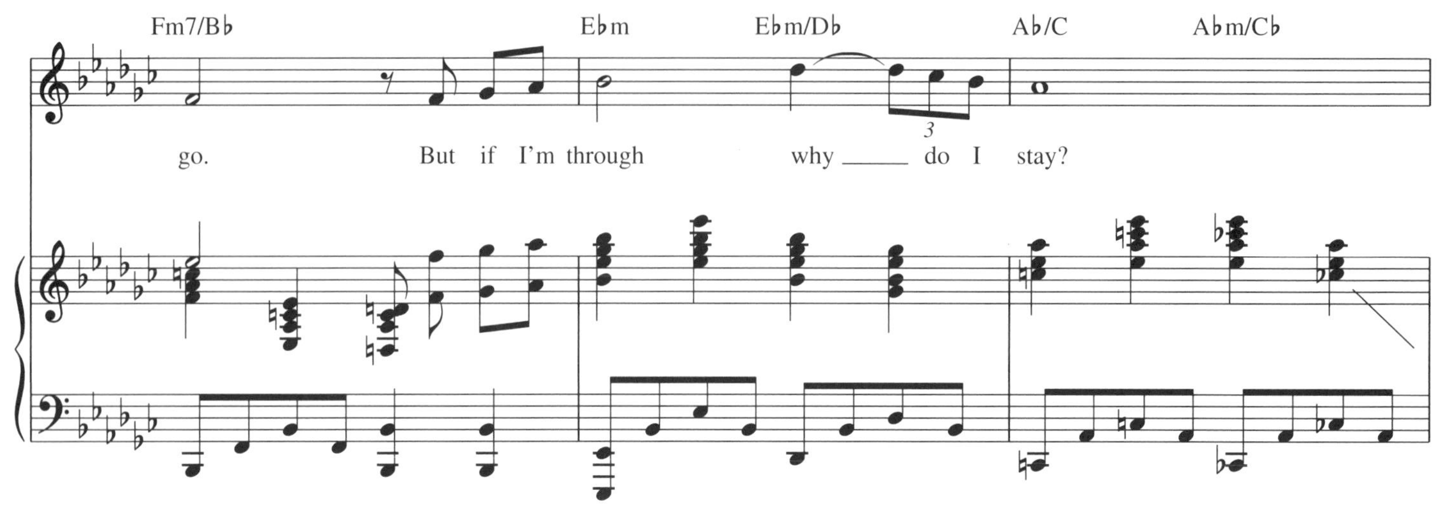
Fm7/B♭
E♭m
E♭m/D♭
A♭/C
A♭m/C♭
go. But if I'm through why ___ do I stay?

Fm7
rit.
May-be he wants me, may-be he needs me, may-be he loves me!
sub.
mp cresc. poco a poco
rit.

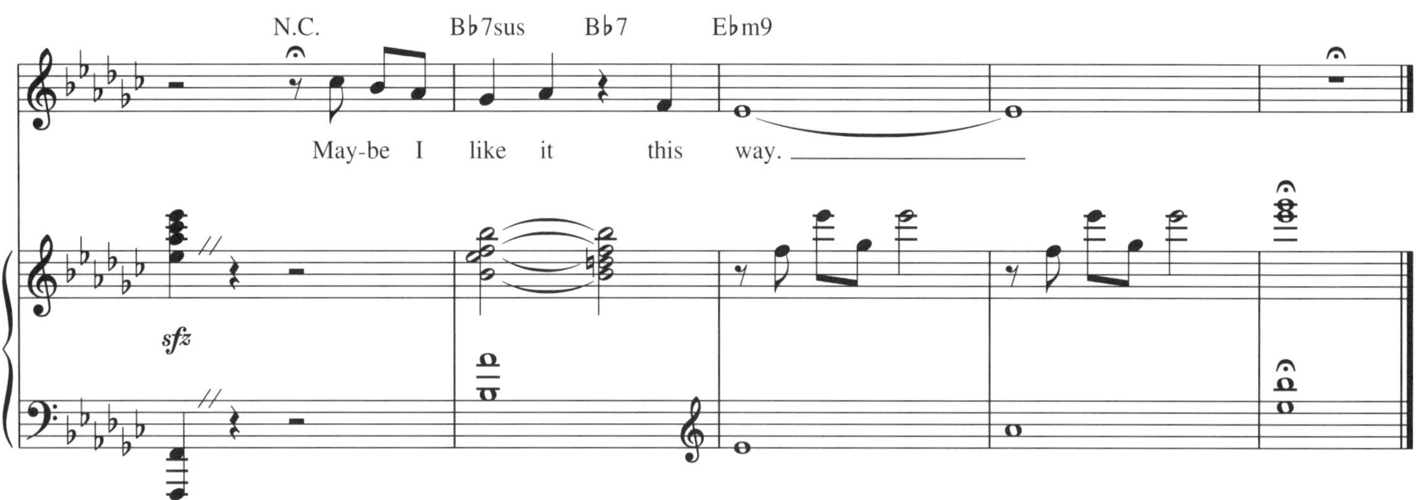
N.C.
B♭7sus
B♭7
E♭m9
May-be I like it this way. ___
sfz

MY BROTHER LIVED IN SAN FRANCISCO

from *Elegies for Angels, Punks and Raging Queens*

Words by BILL RUSSELL
Music by JANET HOOD

Gm7 Dm7 C F(add2) C(add2)/E Am
stark Mon - tan - a skies, and Bud, he seemed to al - ways have
D7sus4 D7/F♯ G7sus4 Em7 Am Em/G
cit - ies in his eyes. He longed for pos - si - bil - i - ty he
3
Fmaj7 D/F♯ C/G Am G F(add2)
lived to move a - way, and he fin - 'lly found his dream in the
C/G B♭(add2) F/A C5
cit - y by the bay.

C(add2)
F(add2)
F
Gm7
Dm7
Joe and I were best of friends in our small-time col-lege
C
F(add2)
F
C(add2)/E
Am
D7sus4
D7/F♯
town, and Joe had per-son-al-i-ty what a cam-pus
G7sus4
Em7
Am
Em/G
Fmaj7
clown. His jokes hid deep-er riv-ers that bub-bled far be-
D/F♯
C/E
Am
G
F(add2)
C/G
low, and he rode the cur-rent west where the rap-id wat-ers

B♭(add2)
A♭
D♭
flow.
Lots of us had
f
cresc.
f
D♭(add2)/C
G♭(add2)/B♭
D♭/A♭
G♭(add2)
broth-ers there who would love to see the sights and share the balm-y
D♭(add2)/F
B♭m7
E♭7sus4
E♭7/G
A♭7sus4
A♭/C
B♭m
free - dom of San Fran-cis-co nights.
They liked it
Fm/A♭
G♭maj7
E♭/G
D♭/A♭
B♭m
A♭
so much more than an - y - where they'd been and we thought they would be

G♭(add2)
D♭/A♭
C♭(add2)
there when we made it back a - gain.
Rubato
B5
B/A♯
E(add2)/G♯
p
My broth - er lived in San Fran - cis - co. He said he fi - n'lly
molto rit.
B/F♯
E(add2)
B/D♯
G♯m
B/F♯
found his place. And when I go to San Fran - cis - co ev - 'ry - where I
F♯7sus4
Emaj7
Amaj7
B5
look I see his face.

NOT FOR THE LIFE OF ME

from *Thoroughly Modern Millie*

Music by JEANINE TESORI
Lyrics by DICK SCANLAN

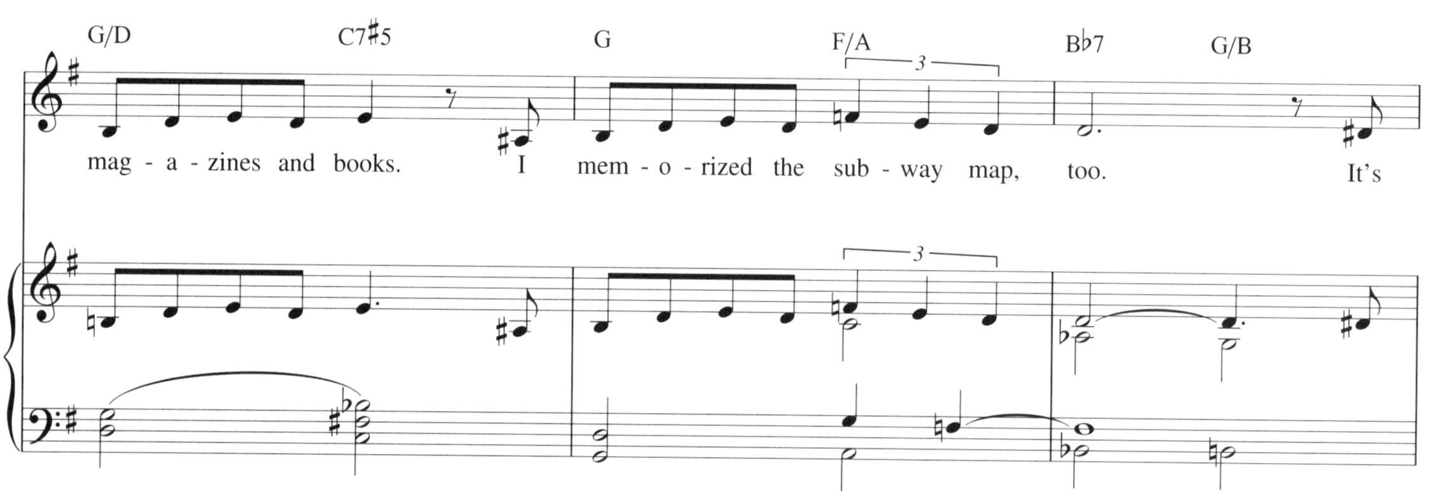

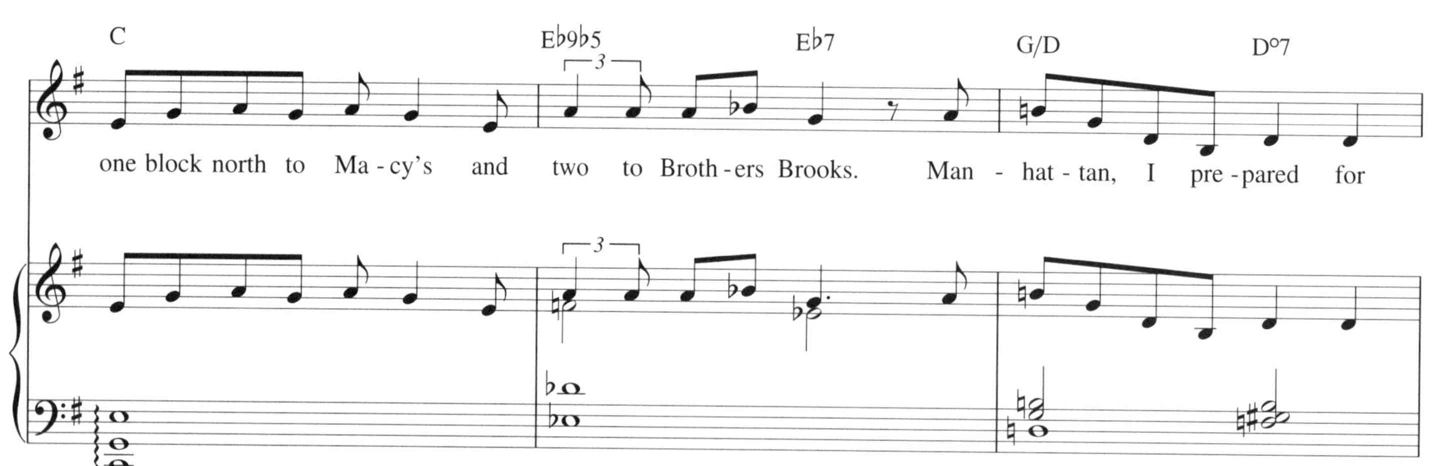

D9sus4 D7♭9 D7 G/D C7 G/D C7♯5
you. You cer - tain - ly are dif - f'rent from what they have back home, where
G F/A B♭7 G/B G7/B C
noth - ing's o - ver three sto - ries high, and no one's in a hur - ry or
E♭9♯11 E♭7 G/D D°7 Am7 D7
wants to roam, but I do, though they won - der why. They
p sub.
B9 B♭7 C/G Am6 B♭7
said I would soon be good and lone - ly. They said I would sing the home - sick
mp

E♭m(add2) E♭m E♭°7 F7/E♭ B♭/D
blues. So I al - ways have this tick - et in my pock - et, a tick - et
F♯m7♭5
Slower
Tacet
A7♭5 E♭7/B♭
home in my pock - et to do with as I choose.
Hot Dixieland
Tacet
A♭6
Tacet
E♭7♯5 A♭7
Burn the bridge. Bet the store. Ba - by's com - in' home
D♭7 B♭7 E♭7 A♭6 B°7
no more. Not for the life of me.

Gm7♭5/B♭
E♭+
A♭
A♭6
Tacet
E♭7♯5
Break the lock. Post my bail.
A♭7
D♭7
B♭7
Done my time, I'm out - ta jail. Not for the
E♭7
A♭
A♭7
A♭°7
B♭m7♭5/A♭
A♭
life of me. A life that's
Em6
B7
Em6
B7
Em6
C7
got - ta be more than a one - light town where the light is al - ways red.
got - ta be more than a coun - try wife mak - in' ba - bies till I croak.

Em6
E7
Got - ta be more _ than an old ghost town where the
Got - ta be more _ than the lead - ing role in a
A7
B♭7
E♭9
ghost ain't e - ven dead.
far - mer's daugh - ter joke.
A♭6
E♭9
Cm7♭5
A♭7
Clap - a - your hands _ just - a - be - cause don't you know that where I am ain't
Days of yore, _ kind and gen - tle, ask me if I'm
D♭7
B♭7
E♭9
where I was. _
sen - ti - men - tal.
Not for the life of

Cm7b5
F7
Bb7
me.
Boh doh dee oh.
Not for the
Not for the
Eb7
1
Ab Ab7 Abo7 Bbm7b5/Ab
Ab
life of
life of,
me.
You see, I
2
Ab7
Db
Do7
Ab/Eb
E7
not for the life of,
not for the life
Eb9
Ab
Bb
Ab7#5
D(b5)
Ab
of
me!
L.H.

NOTHING REALLY HAPPENED

from the Broadway Musical *Is There Life After High School?*

Music and Lyric by
CRAIG CARNELIA

Esus
E(no5)
Esus
E(no5)
- ly e - ven hap - pened.
poco rit.
Esus
E
F♯m7(addB)
We talked some truth, we told some lies.
espres.
a tempo
G♯m(addE)
F♯m7(addB)
E
He pushed the hair
F♯m7(addB)
G♯m(addE)
F♯m7(addB)
a - way from my eyes.

E
F♯m7(addB)
G♯m(addE)
It felt so dan - ger - ous then, and noth - ing real -
F♯m7(addB)
E
F♯m7(addB)
- ly e - ven hap - pened.
cresc.
G♯m(addE)
F♯m7(addB)
E
Fun - ny, the things you think
mf Rock ballad feel
Bm7(no5)
E
E7sus
a - bout. Fun - ny, the things you don't.

Amaj7
Adim
C♯m7(no5)
Fun-ny, the things that fade a - way.
Fun - ny, the things that won't.
C6(no5)
E
F♯m7(addB)
The girl I tried so hard to hide.
espres.
rit.
a tempo
mp
G♯m(addE)
F♯m7
E
The wom - an wak-
F♯m7(addB)
G♯m(addE)
F♯m7
- ing up in - side.

E
F#m7(addB)
G#m(addE)
(add7)
The way I pic - tured his bed.
The scenes I saw
mf
E7sus
Amaj7
Adim
in my head.
Wonder if I should write him.
f
E
E7sus
Amaj7
Won-der if I should call.
Won-der if he'd re-mem-
Adim
E
Emaj9
E
E7sus
- ber at all.
I

Amaj7
Adim
C♯m7
wonder if he'd remember at all.
mf
mp
C6
C♯m7(no5)
Cmaj7(no5)
C6(no5)
rall.
E
F♯m7(addB)
G♯m(addE)
A million years ago tonight
mp a tempo
F♯m7(addB)
E
F♯m7(addB)
the T. V. glowed in black and white.

G♯m(addE)
F♯m7(addB)
E
And I re - mem -
ber that girl,
that girl a - lone with that boy.
poco rit.
a tempo
poco rit.
And I re - mem - ber that night,
that night when noth -
a tempo
poco rit.
a tempo
rit.
B7sus(no5)
F♯
Am/C
ing real - ly hap - pened.
a tempo
rit.

STILL HURTING

from *The Last Five Years*

Music and Lyrics by
JASON ROBERT BROWN

C F/A B♭2 C F/A B♭2
Ja-mie ar-rived at the end of the line. Ja-mie's con-vinced that the prob-lems are
mp flowing
C Dmin7 C/E D7/F♯ E7/G♯
mine. Ja-mie is prob-a-bly feel-ing just fine, And
F2/A B♭2 G7/B Csus C Dmin11 C2/E F6/9 Csus C C/B
I'm still hurt - ing.
sub. p
mp
Amin9 F2 Amin9
What a-bout lies, Ja - mie? What a-bout things That you swore to be true?
mf legato

D9/F♯
F2
C/E
Dmin11
G(add 11)
What a-bout you, Ja-mie? What a-bout you?
p
C
F/A
B♭2
C
Ja-mie is sure some-thing won-der-ful died.
mp
C
F/A
B♭2
C
Ja-mie de-cides it's his right to de-cide.
Dmin7
C/E
D7/F♯
E7/G♯
Ja-mie's got se-crets he does-n't con-fide, And

F2/A
B♭2
G7/B
Csus
I'm still hurt - ing.
(sempre mf)
molto cresc.
E♭/C
D/C
D♭/C
C
G/B
Go and hide and run a - way! Run a-way,
f
Amin7
D9
F6/9
run and find some - thing bet - ter!
mf
D♭/E♭
F/E♭
E/E♭
E♭
Go and ride the sun a - way! Run a-way,
f

Cmin7
A♭2
Fmin11
like it's simple, Like it's right...
mf
mp
C
F/A
B♭2
C
F/A
B♭2
3
C
Dmin7
C/E
D/F♯
E7/G♯
F/A
B♭
G7/B
Csus
5
mf
Amin9
F2
Give me a day, Ja - mie! Bring back the lies, Hang them
8va

Amin9
D9/F♯
4
F2
C/E
back on the wall!
May-be I'd see
How you could be
So cer-tain that
mp
Cmin7/E♭
D♭Maj11
G(add 11)
we Had no chance
at all.
C
F/A
B♭2
C
F/A
B♭2
Ja-mie is o - ver and where can I turn?
Cov-ered with scars I did no-thing to earn?
pp
C
Dmin7
C/E
D7/F♯
E7/G♯
May-be there's some-where a les-son to learn,
But

F2/A
Gsus/B
F2/A
that would-n't change the fact,
That would-n't speed the time,
mf
Gsus/B
F2/A
Emin7
Once the foun - da - tion's cracked
And
F2
G(add 11)
I'm
Still
mf
colla voce
C
F/A
B♭2
C
rit.
F/A
B♭2
C
hurt - ing.
mp

TAKE THE WORLD AWAY

from *Little by Little*

Music by BRAD ROSS
Lyric by ELLEN GREENFIELD

Ballad

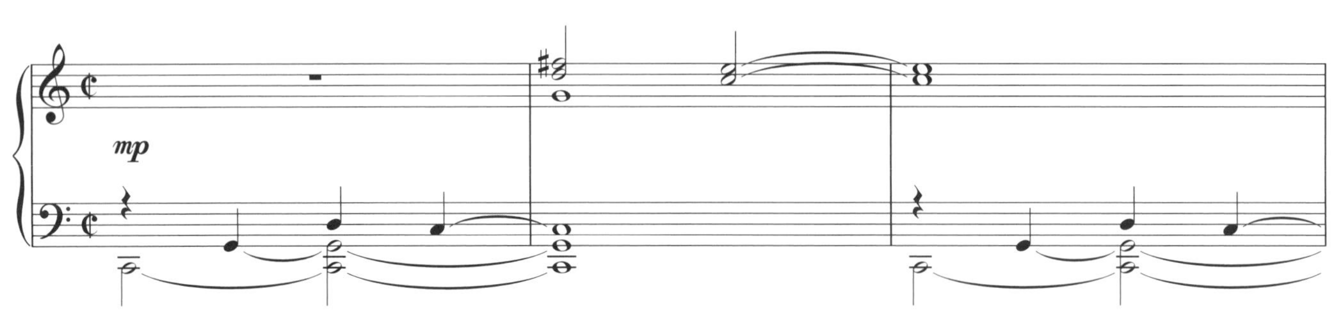

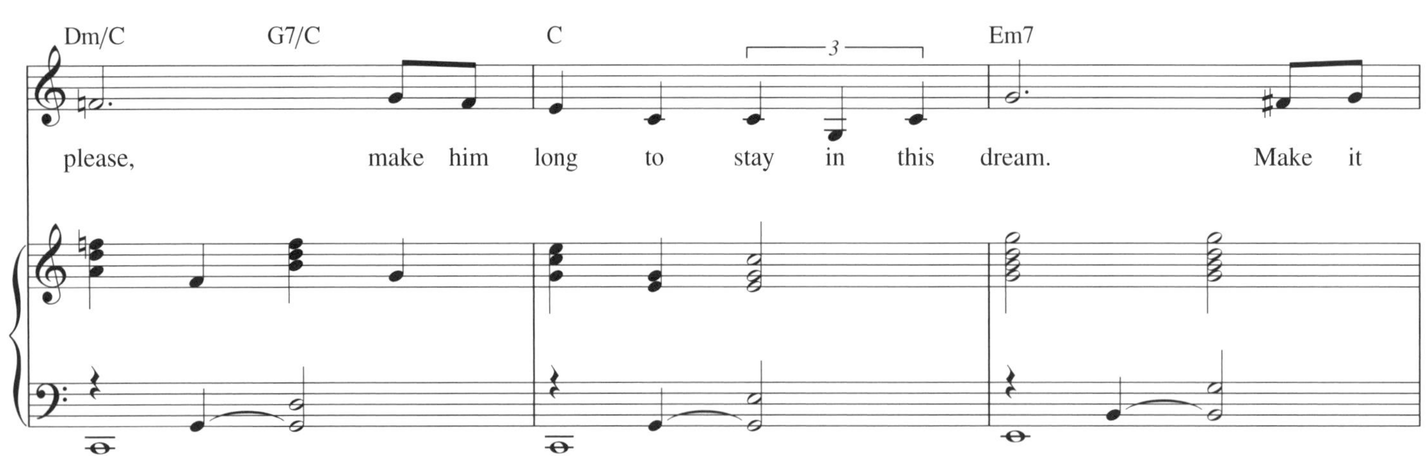

A7sus A7 Dm7 G7 C(add2)
last, I pray. Take the world a - way. Oh

C D/C Dm/C
please, for a sin - gle night, oh please, can't I

C Em7 Asus A7
3
have the right to do wrong? How I wish I might take the

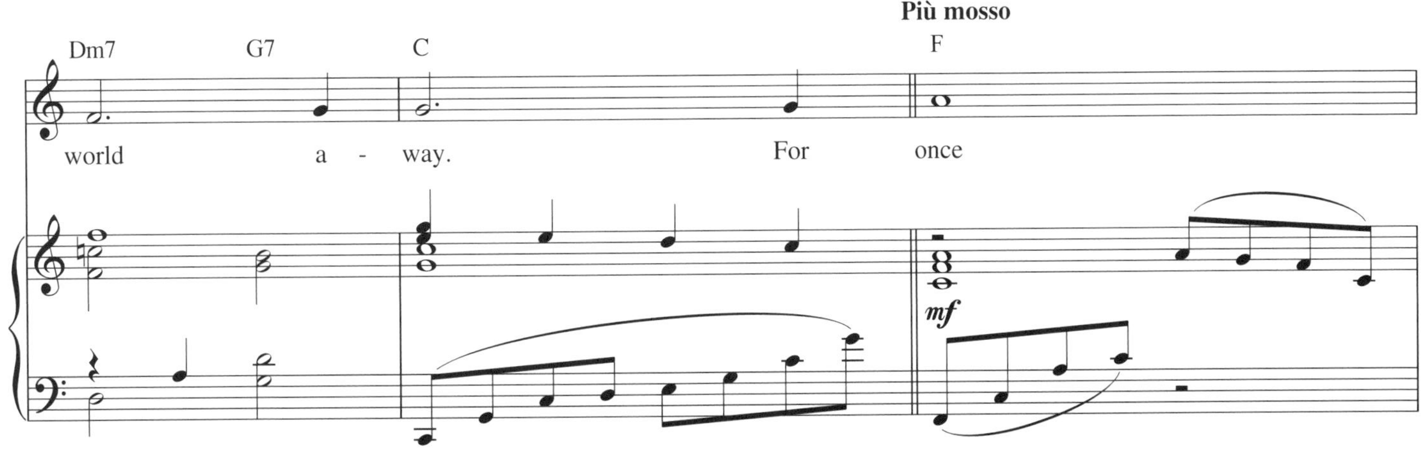
Più mosso
Dm7 G7 C F
world a - way. For once
mf

C/E
can't I once be rash and wild? For
E♭
once be a reck - less
B♭/D
fool?
B♭/D
For
D♭
once can't he read my
F/C
F/B♭
mind?
F/A
F/G
Can't I take the
D7/F♯
C/E
lead,
cresc.

D7
Dm7/G
G7
let my pas - sions rule?
Oh
f
rit.
p
C(add2)
D/C
Dm7/C
please, if it's meant to be, oh please, let him
C(add2)
Em7
Bm7/E
E7
3
look and see all my dreams are of him with
mf
f
Am
Am/G
Dm7
G7sus
me.
Take the world a -
ff
p
quicker

Gm7/C
C7
F(add2)
Am7/E
C/D
way. Oh please, make to - day the day.
move
D7
Dm7
Dm7/G
G7
Take the world a -
L.H.
rit.
L.H.
rit.
C
D/C
D♭/C
way.
a little faster
f
C
Cmaj9
8va
mp
faster
rit.
L.H.
p

THERE'S A FINE, FINE LINE

from the Broadway Musical *Avenue Q*

Music and Lyrics by ROBERT LOPEZ
and JEFF MARX

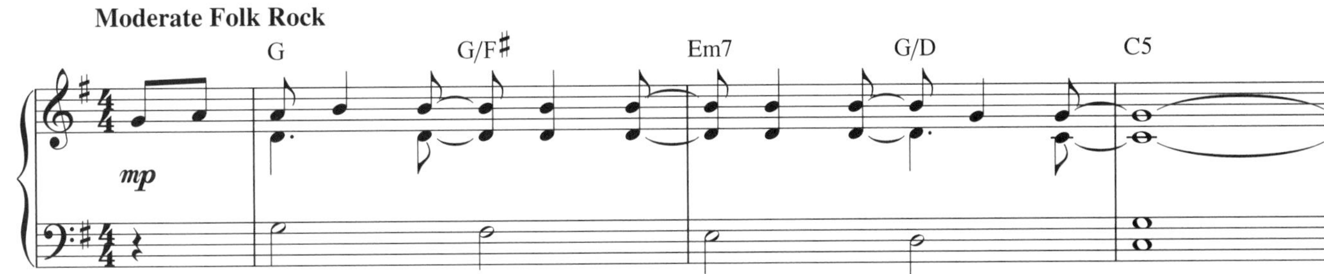

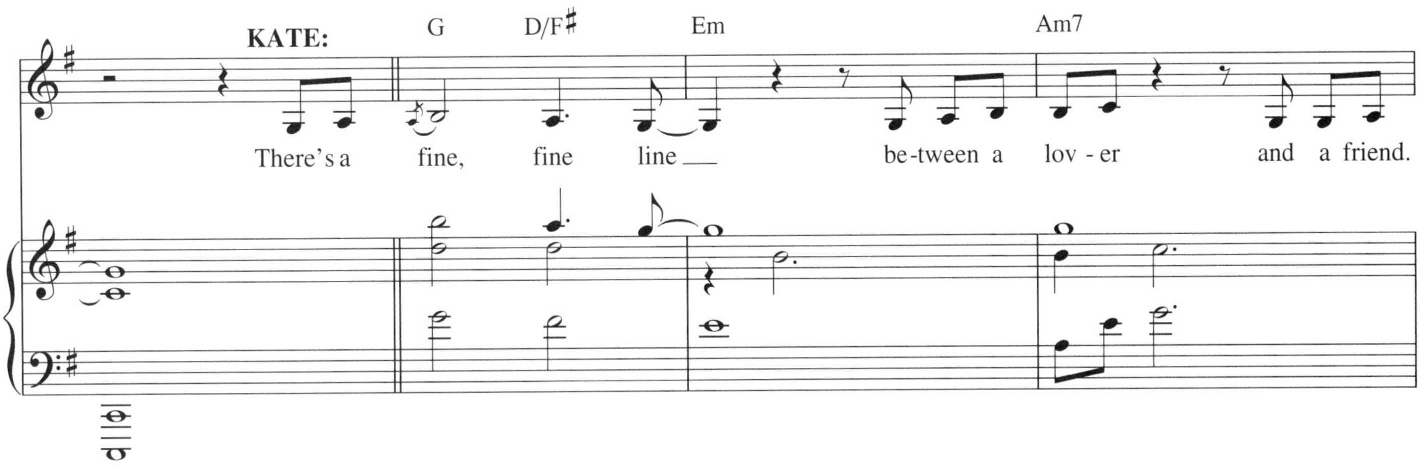

Cm G D/F♯ Em7 G/D Cmaj7
There's a fine, fine line be - tween love
D7sus G G/B Cmaj7 D5 G D/F♯
and a waste of time. There's a fine, fine line
8vb
Em Am7 D7sus D7 G D/F♯
be-tween a fair-y tale and a lie. And there's a fine, fine line
Em Am7 D7sus D7 G D/F♯
be-tween "you're won-der-ful" and "good-bye." I guess if some-one does - n't love

Em7 Bm7/D Cmaj7 Cm G D/F♯
you back, it is-n't such a crime, but there's a fine, fine line
3
8vb
Em7 G/D Cmaj7 D7sus G G/B
be-tween love and a waste of your time.
Cmaj7 D D/C G/B
And I don't have the time to waste on you an-y-more.
cresc.
f
8vb
G D Em7 D A/C♯ D G
I don't think that you e-ven know what you're look-ing for.
8vb

G D/F♯ Em7 D E
E/D
C♯m7
For my own san - i - ty, I've got to close the door
8vb
F♯m F♯m/E
D
D7/C
Bm
and walk a - way...
Whoa...
dim.
mp
dim.
mp
D7(no3)
G D/F♯
Em
Am7
There's a fine, fine line be-tween to - geth - er and not.
D7sus D7
G D/F♯
Em
Am7
And there's a fine, fine line be-tween what you want-ed and what you
3

D
C/D
D
G
G/F♯
got.
You got - ta go af - ter the things
Em7
G/D
Cmaj7
Cm
E♭
F/E♭
E♭
you want while you're still in your prime...
Broader
F/E♭
F
G
G/F♯
Em7
G/D
C
Cmaj7
There's a fine, fine line be-tween love
rit.
8vb
poco rit.
8vb
D7(no3)
G
G/B
Cmaj7
D7
G
and a waste of time.
rit.
8vb

TEACHING THIRD GRADE

from *Ruthless*

Lyric by JOEL PALEY
Music by MARVIN LAIRD

Rubato
Eb7b5(b9)
Eb7
Abmaj7(add2,6)
Dbmaj7/Eb
Teach-ing third grade
Shap-ing the minds of a
Abmaj9
Dbmaj7/Eb
Abmaj7(add2,6)
Dbmaj7/Eb
E9/D# Eb9
new gen-er-a-tion
No lon-ger a-fraid
to get on with my life and
Moderate 2
Ebm9
Ebm7
Ab7b9
Dbmaj7
C7/Ab Db(add2)
off med-i-ca-tion
Sure, I went to New York to be an
Dbm9
Gb9(add6)
E9
Abmaj7/Eb
Ab+/E
Fm9
o-ver night sen-sa-tion
More than a face I was a

B♭7(add6)
E9
win - ning com - bin - a - tion of tal - ent and grace
A♭maj7/E♭
Fm7
I should-'a packed mace 'cause I was
B♭9
A♭/C
A♭+/D♭
B♭9/D
E9(add6)
E♭9sus
mugged, raped and robbed be-fore I left Penn Sta - tion
B♭m7sus/E♭
B♭m7♭5/E♭
E♭7sus
E♭9sus
Now I'm back, Lord, at the black - board teach-ing third grade.
8vb

(𝅗𝅥 = ♩)
Cm/A♭
E7/G♯
Some-thing to fall back on
Sure, it works for some
But
8va
A♭maj7
E♭m9
D♭maj9 D♭maj7 D♭maj9 D♭maj7
I fell back and look what life's be - come
To - night I'll get co - zy, Pour
G♭13♯11
Fm9
A♭+/C A♭/F
A♭/B♭
B♭9♭5
B♭9
wine, light the ta - pers Then sit there a-lone there all night grad-ing pa - pers
D♭/E♭
D♭+
E♭/D♭
Cm7sus4 A♭/C Cm7 F13♭9
A♭9/B♭
Cm7sus4
The pay may be stea-dy My sum - mer's are free
But do you want your daugh-ter to

Dbmaj9
Eb7sus4
Eb7b5
Eb7
Eb7#5/A
Abmaj7
turn out like me Yeah, I had some-thing to fall back on
E7/G#
Abmaj7
Gb13#11
F7sus4
Safe and so se-cure With ve-ry few sur-pris-es in store This
8va
Bbm9
Bdim
Cm7
F7b9(add6)
Eb7sus4/Bb
Cm7
chee-ry de-mea-nor It's all a cha-rade The truth is I'm bored I hate
(8va)
Double-time feel
Dbmaj9
Emaj7
teach-ing third grade
(8va)

Bb(no3)
Abmaj7/Bb
Sick of Jane and sick of Dick-ie, Nev-er qui-et, al-ways stick-y
Db/Eb
Db+/Eb
Nos-es run-ny, nos-es bleed-y, Lit-tle runts so blood-y need-y,
Dmaj7/E
Dmaj7#5/E
Joan hits Jan-ice with a slink-ey
Bart makes Ter-ry touch his wink-ie
E9
G6/E
This one cried
and that one peed

E13
3
Dm6/E
I can't take it God, I need
Amaj7
Dm6/A
Some-thing to fall back on
Amaj7
from what I've fal - len back on
Dm6/A
D6/E
As

Moderato
A
E7/A
far as the lead in the show my dear She'll
A
A6(add2)
E/G♯
have to get o - ver not win - ning this year
Em9♭5/G
D/F♯
A/E
In - to each life rain falls I'm a - fraid Life is a bitch
poco rit.
rall.
E9sus
A
D/E
A
And it starts in third grade.
ten.
ten.
mf
f

TOO BEAUTIFUL FOR WORDS

from the Broadway Musical *The Color Purple*

Words and Music by ALLEE WILLIS, BRENDA RUSSELL and STEPHEN BRAY

guess that means that you are just too beau - ti - ful for words. I
A tempo - Slow 4
seen this life from high and low, and all that's in - be - tween. I
danced with dukes, crooned with counts, been court - ed like a queen. But
when I see what's in your heart, all the past is blurred. The

grace you bring in - to this world's too beau - ti - ful for words. You
hide your head un - der your wings just like a lit - tle bird.
Oh don't you know you're beau - ti - ful, too beau - ti - ful for words.
mf
dim.
p
rit.
Oo, Ce - lie, you're too beau - ti - ful for words.
opt. Oo,

WHEN YOU GOT IT, FLAUNT IT

from *The Producers*

Music and Lyrics by
MEL BROOKS

Moderate Swing

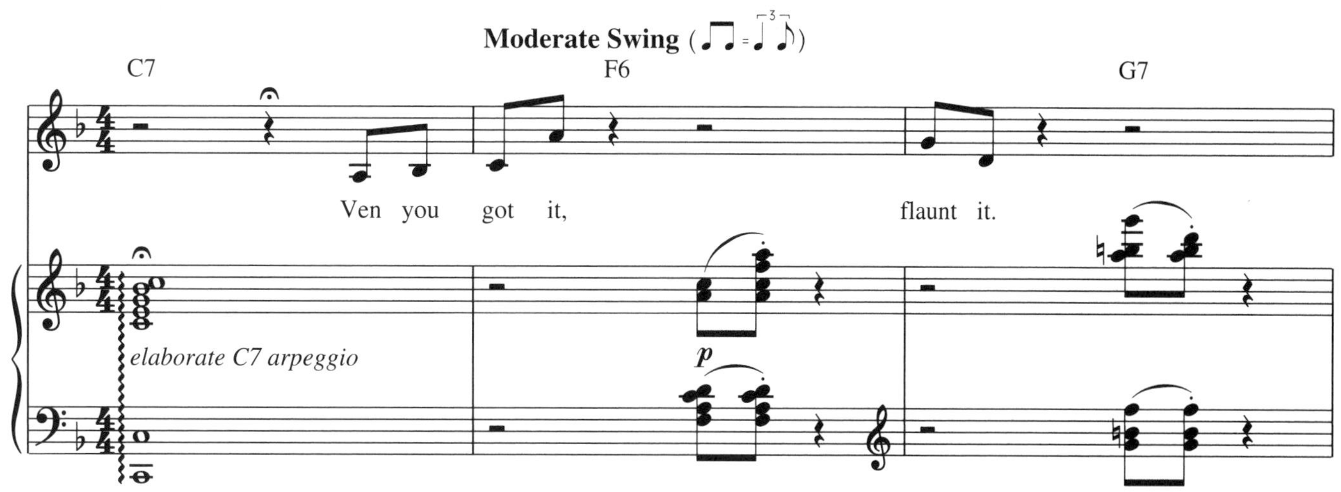

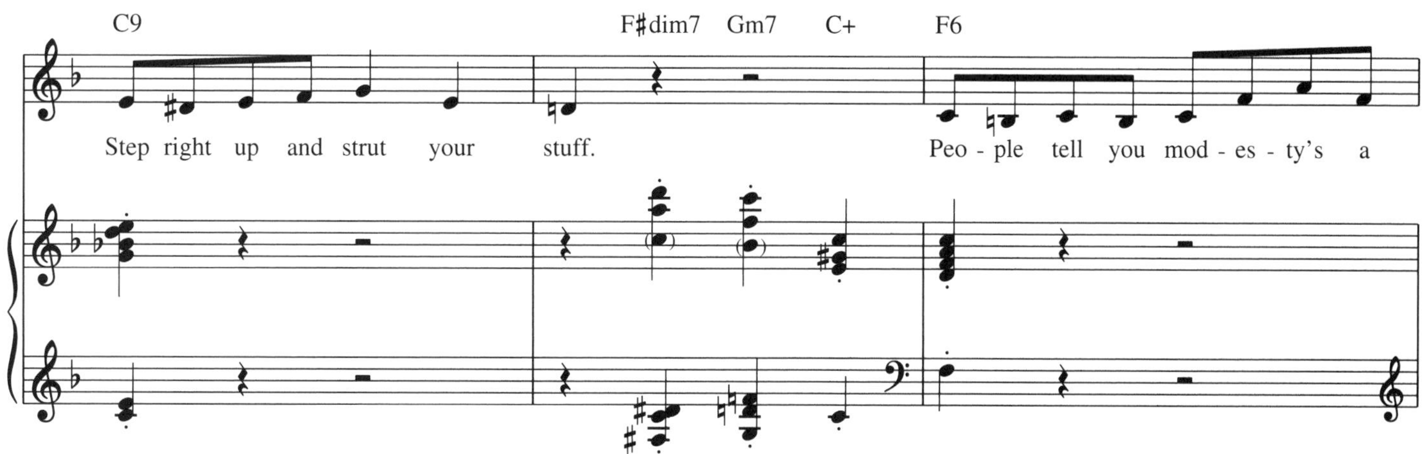

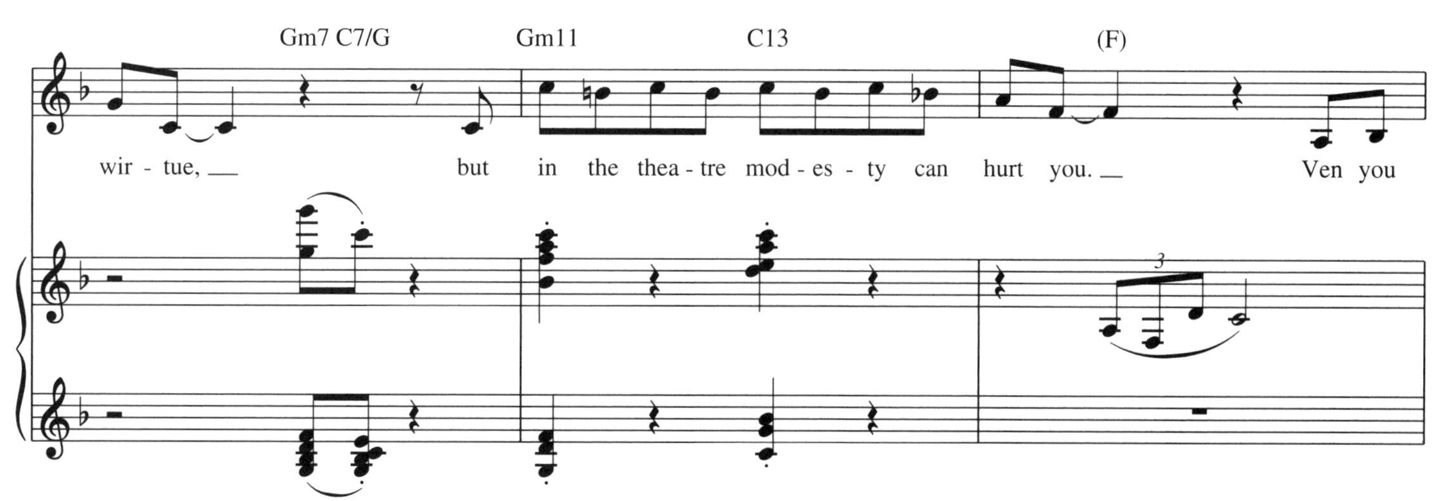

F6/C
G9/D
C7
got it,
flaunt it.
Show your as - sets let 'em know you're
mp
Em7
A7
D9
G13
proud.
Your
good - ies you must push,
stick your
chest out, shake your tush,
ven you
F6/C
G9/C
C7♭9
F6
Gm7/C
Cool Swing
F
got it,
shout it out
loud!
Ven you got it
mf
mp
G
C7
F6
F♯dim7
C13
show it
put your hid - den trea - sures on dis - play

F6/9
Gm7
C9
Gm9
C11
Vi - o - lin - ists love to play an E - string _ But au - di - enc - es real - ly love a
F/A
G♯dim7
Gm7
C13
F6
G7
G - string _ Ven you got it, ___ shout it. ___
mf
C7
A7
D7
Let the whole vorld hear vat you're a - bout Clothes may make the man, all a
G7
Gm9
D♭7♯5
C13
F6
girl needs is a tan ven you got it let ___ it hang out. _______ Ven

Sweetly
Em7♭5 A7 Dm A7♭9/D Dm Em7♭5 A7
straight 8ths
I was yust a lit - tle girl in Sve - den my thought - ful mo - ther gave me this ad -
mp
Dm Dm7 G7 C6 Am7
vice: If na - ture bles - ses you from top to bot - tom,
8va
6
Swing!
Dm11 G13 C13
show that top to bot - tom, don't think twice. Don't think
3
mf
Ab♭m9/D♭ D♭13 A♭m/D♭ B♭m/C♭ C♭/B♭ D♭/A♭
twice. Ven you
f
3

Broad swing
G6 G6/F♯ Em7 G6/D A13 A13/G A13/F♯ A13/E
got it ___ share it. ___
ff
D7 D9 G6 E7/G♯ Am7 D9
Let the pub - lic feast up - on your charms.
G G/F♯ Em7 G/D Am11 D7 Am11 D13
Peo - ple say that be - ing prim is prop - er, ___ But ev - 'ry show-girl knows that "prim" will
mf
G E♭9 A♭ A♭/G Fm9 A♭/E♭
stop her. ___ Ven you got it, ___
f

B♭7
E♭7
B♭m/D♭
give it.
Don't be self - ish, give it all a -
C7
B♭add9/D
E♭dim7
C7/E
vay!
Don't be
F7
shy, be bold and cute,
show the
p
ff
B♭9♭5
boys that birth - day suit
ven you
p
ff

"Going home"
Bbm9
got it
If you got it
Dbm7
got it
f
Once you got it
Ab6/Eb
Bb9/Eb
Eb13
shout out hoo -
gliss.
Samba-straight 8ths
Eb7
ray!
ff
Ab
Ab/Gb
Db/F
Dbm/Fb
Eb7sus
Ab6/9
fff

WHO WEARS THESE CLOTHES?

from *The Times*

Music by BRAD ROSS
Lyric by JOE KEENAN

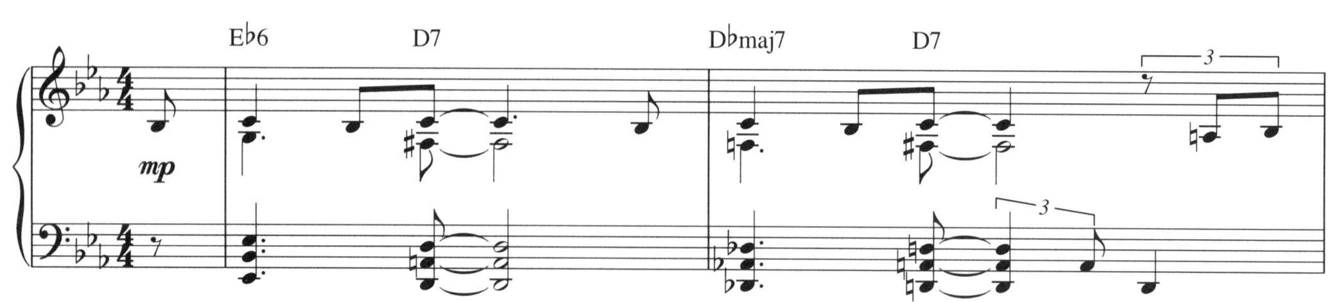

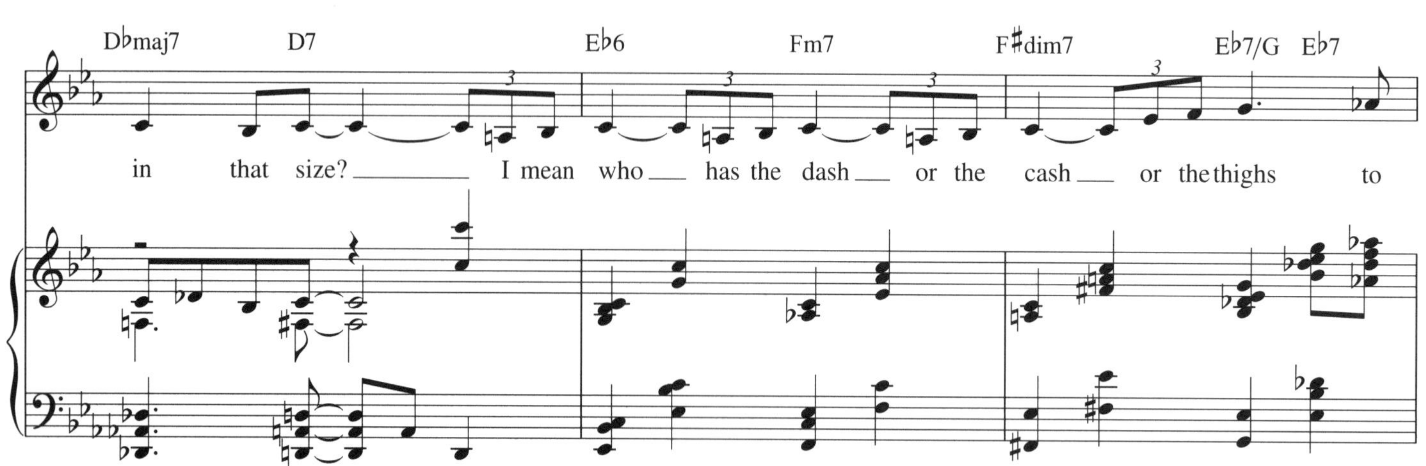

A♭maj9
D♭13
C13
F13
F(♭13)
buy such a gown? Sup - pose that you'd dare it, Sup - pose you look fair. O - kay
F7
F7(♭5)
A♭/B♭
Gm7
C7
where do you wear it? The flesh it bares. And what if it tears? Who
Fm7
B♭13
B♭(♭13)
E♭6
D7
wears these clothes? Who looks like that? It's
D♭maj7
D7
E♭6
Fm7
more than clothes It's the straight lit - tle nose the com - plex - ion that glows and the

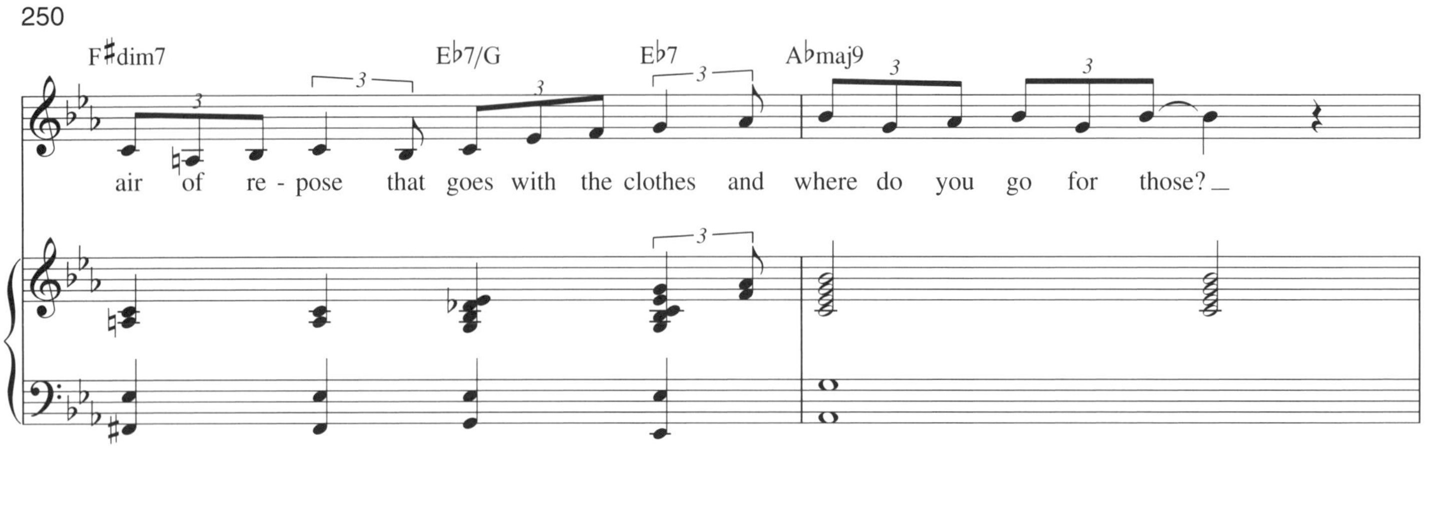
F♯dim7
E♭7/G
E♭7
A♭maj9
air of re - pose that goes with the clothes and where do you go for those?

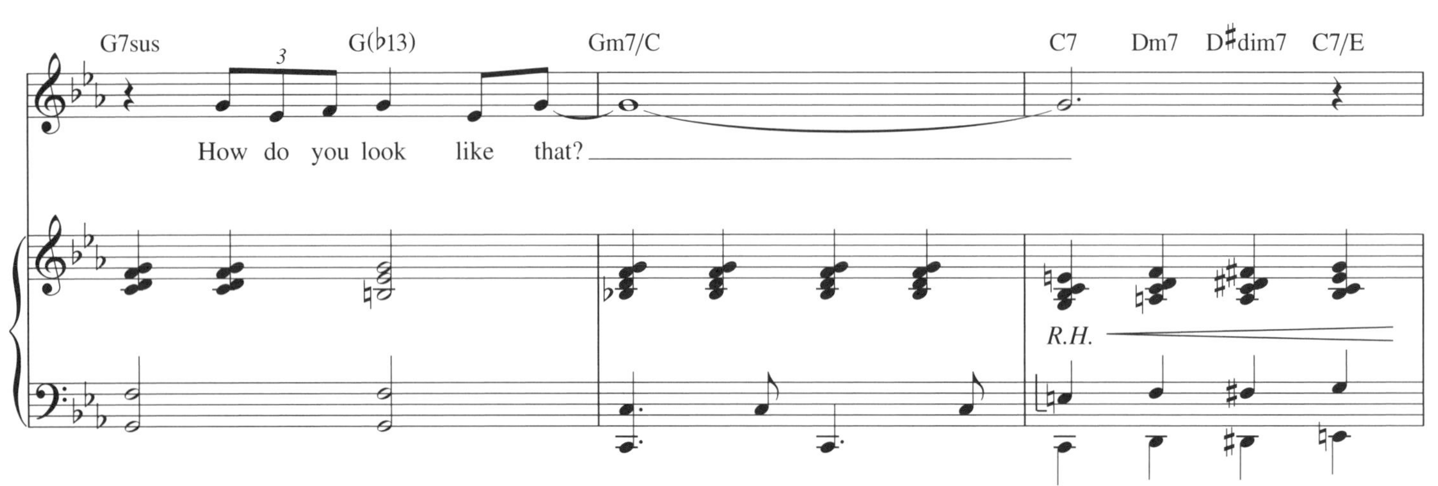
G7sus
G(♭13)
Gm7/C
C7
Dm7
D♯dim7
C7/E
How do you look like that?
R.H.

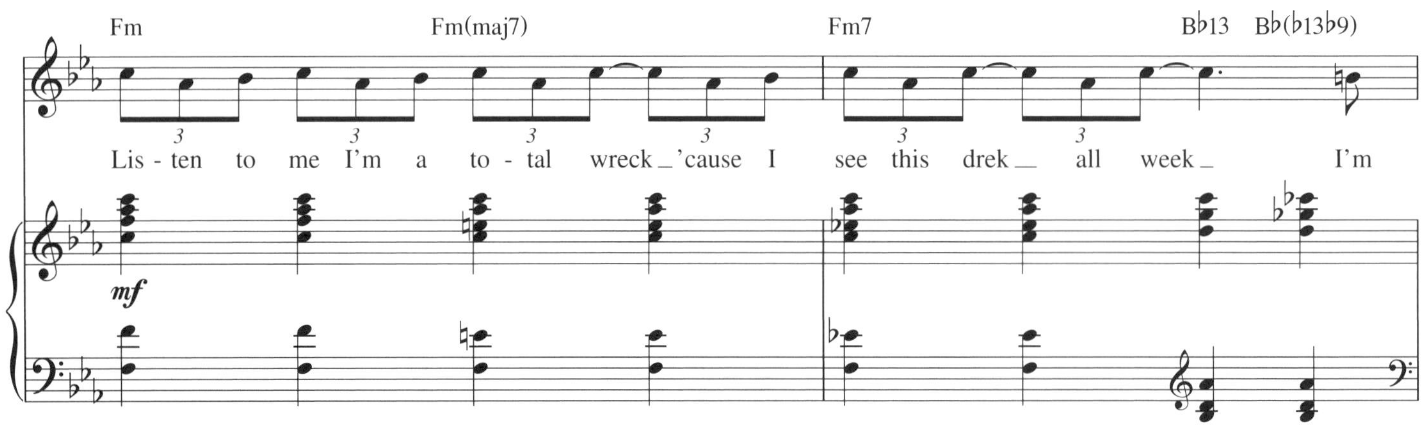
Fm
Fm(maj7)
Fm7
B♭13
B♭(♭13♭9)
Lis - ten to me I'm a to - tal wreck 'cause I see this drek all week I'm
mf

E♭(add2)
Gm7(♭5)/D♭
C7
B♭m/D
E♭m
C7/E
me - di - a wise and look fine for my size and my clothes are all pass - a - bly chic I

A♭m
A♭m♯5
A♭m6
D♭7
jog and I swim and I go to the gym and I watch ev - 'ry mor - sel and meal Then I
G♭
Fm11
B♭7
E♭6
D7
look at these girls and I feel like a hunch - back. To wear these clothes, to
8va
sfz
sfz
8vb
D♭maj7
D7
E♭6
Fm7
F♯dim7
E♭13
D♭/E♭
live that role, to be seen in that hat look - ing that in con - trol, to
Alternate Lyric: they
A♭maj9
D♭13
dress like a dream and to seem so su - preme - ly in
thrill, they pro - voke but they're sort of a joke in size

C7
B♭/D
E♭dim
C7/E
charge.
three.
I could
Fm7
F♯dim7
Gm7
play the swan, but the world would scoff 'cause you don't put on what you
f
Build to harder swing
C13
C(♭13)
Fm7
can't pull off. Who wears these clothes?
8va
ff
A♭/B♭
A♭maj7/B♭
B♭9
D♭6
D6
D♭6
D6
E♭6
Alternate Lyric:
And where do you find them in large?
Well, God on - ly knows it ain't me!
(8va)
sfz
8vb

YOU DON'T KNOW THIS MAN

from *Parade*

Music and Lyrics by
JASON ROBERT BROWN

You don't know this man.
poco animato
rit.
p a tempo
You don't e - ven try.
When a man writes his
poco accel. e cresc.
moth-er ev-'ry Sun-day, pays his bills be-fore they're due, works so hard to feed his fam-'ly, there's your
poco accel. e cresc.
mur-der-er for you! And you stand here spit-ting words that you know aren't true. Then
allarg.

mf
you don't know this man. I don't think you
mf a tempo
could. You don't have the right to know a
f
man that wise and good. He is a de - cent man!
rall.
f a tempo
mf
He is an hon - est man! And you don't
p
sub. p colla voce
mf a tempo
sub. p

Tempo primo
mf
mp
know…
And you nev - er
will.
Not from me, not from an - y - one who knows him, not a
mor - sel, not a crumb, not a clue.
Freely
pp
I have
noth - ing more to say to you.
pp
poco rit.
p a tempo
rit.
pp